COMMERCIAL REAL ESTATE

The Ultimate Beginner's Guide for Learning the Effective Ways in Commercial Real Estate

Table of Contents

Introduction

Commercial real estate investment is fast becoming a popular choice of career path for ambitious people. In the past, real estate investors used to shy away from commercial real estate investments because it was regarded as being complicated, difficult, and complex, but this was nothing more than a myth. Now that this myth about commercial real estate has been unraveled, many investors like you are looking to learn more about buying, leasing, and selling of commercial real estate so they can start making steady income like all the commercial real estate investors they know. However, no matter how hard they try, there seem to be no resource(s) that offer the information they need.

If you are currently reading this introduction, congratulations; you are one of the lucky commercial real estate enthusiasts who are privileged to be reading this ultimate guide to successful commercial real estate investment. "Commercial Real Estate: The Ultimate Beginners Guide to Learning the Effective Ways in Commercial Real Estate" has been written to be a comprehensive, detailed, self-explanatory, and absolute guide for people who are new to the commercial real estate industry. This book proves itself as a credible source of authentic commercial real estate knowledge by employing the use of expressive words, simple language, and a breakdown of the most technical aspect of commercial real estate to educate even the most clueless reader on everything relating to how to be a successful real estate investor, beginner or no beginner. In the book, readers will broadly learn about varying commercial real estate knowledge that is critical to effective investment in commercial real estate.

First, you will be learning in detail the basic knowledge about commercial real estate, how it differs from residential real estate investment, and the many investment opportunities waiting for you in the commercial property market. Next, you will also be intimated with everything you require to get started with commercial real estate with the most common technical terms to familiarize yourself with broken down into very simple language for you. We will also look at a range of very important commercial real estate topics ranging from securing a deal and financing the deal to how to fill up your commercial property with the best-paying tenants you will find in and around your local area so you can start generating a steady and consistent source of income. More importantly, you will be taught how to evaluate and appraise a property's value in a step-by-step manner with the use of important evaluation metrics. Aside from these, there are plenty more things you stand to gain from reading this guide from start to finish.

Commercial real estate for beginners is a book that promises to deliver on everything that will help you kick-start your commercial real estate career and also give you tips with which you can propel yourself to the top of the commercial investment game. If you have been thirsting for practical information that will be of immense help to your commercial real estate venture, then this is the right time for you to pick up a copy of this book. Grab a seat, and start reading your way to commercial real estate investment success!

Chapter 1

Understanding Commercial Real Estate

Real estate is one of the best ways to generate passive income and build wealth. Investing in commercial real estate particularly can become an individual's highest source of income when done correctly, but many people, including you, probably do not know this or they have no idea where to start commercial real estate from. This is exactly why we are going to break down the commercial real estate investment right from the very beginning to the end to help you understand what this goldmine is all about. Before we go move ahead, though, let's answer the question, "What is commercial real estate?".

According to investor.com, commercial real estate is any property that is exclusively used for business activity. In other words, commercial real estate is any property that is usually leased out for retail and business purposes only. That exactly is where the difference between commercial real estate and residential real estate lies. While residential real estate is any property that contains a single or multi-family structure that may not be used for commercial or industrial purpose, commercial real estate is leased out specifically for commercial and business purposes only. Note that industrial real estate is not the same as commercial real estate.

Therefore, a commercial real estate investor purchases or singlehandedly develops property that has been solely designed for the purpose of housing commercial tenants. Commercial real estate investment involves the leasing out of this purchased property to businesses that in turn pay rent for the space they are occupying in the property.

There are lots of opportunities in the real estate industry for a commercial real estate investor because we can find commercial property all around us and there are several people ready, waiting for a property or part of it to be leased out to them. It is pertinent that you know exactly what kind of property counts as commercial real estate before you get out there and start fishing around for investment opportunities. Understanding the different types of commercial real estate property will provide you with better insights into what kind of property you should invest or specialize in. Commercial properties are used for a wide range of purposes, but typically, they can be categorized into five different types and these are:

- Office
- Retail
- Industrial
- Multi-family
- Special purpose

The **office** is the most common commercial property and also the most commonly invested in among commercial real estate investors. Buildings that provide office space usually range from single-tenant office spaces to skyscrapers and they are described by either of these categories: Class A, Class B, or Class C.

Class A commercial properties are defined as those buildings that have just been newly designed or extensively renovated, located in the choicest part of the areas which have easy access to all the major amenities. These buildings are normally handled by professional real estate management companies. Class B commercial properties, on the other hand, are properties that include older buildings that need some form of renovation which require capital investment. These buildings are usually well-managed and maintained but they still need minor upgrades and a little touch here and there and they are the common targets for commercial real estate investors. Class C commercial real estate properties that are the last class are buildings, which are purchased for redevelopment opportunities. These properties are typically located in poorly developed areas with little or no amenities and a commercial real estate investor would have to invest some major capital into upgrading the outdated infrastructure. Also, Class C office buildings normally have a higher vacancy rates than Class A and Class B.

Next is the **retail,** which is the most common type of commercial real estate after the office. Retail properties always range from shopping malls to restaurants, banks, and community retail centers are often located in the metropolitan part of the city. In fact, the properties size can extend from a little 5,000 square feet to as much as 350,000 square feet.

Although **Industrial** is mostly classified as industrial real estate, it may be categorized under commercial real estate too since it is used majorly for the purpose of business. Industrial properties range from small warehoused to the larger manufacturing sites. However, they typically tilt towards manufacturing sites because of the availability of spaces with height specifications and docking.

Multifamily commercial properties include buildings with apartment complexes, high-rise condos, and multifamily units. Now, you may wonder if this isn't residential real estate since it is meant for living. However, a property could count as multifamily real estate if it has just a single unit. With more than four units though, this property can be categorized as a commercial real estate property. Most residential real estate investors get started in commercial real estate investment by investing capitals in larger multifamily properties, which count as commercial real estate.

Finally, **special purpose** commercial properties are the building that are designed for a specific purpose, meaning it may be impossible or difficult to use it for any reason than that specified purpose. Examples are car washes, schools, self-storage facilities, etc. A large portion of the special purpose real estate fall under the tourism and leisure industry and the common examples you already know are airports, hotels, stadium, resorts, amusement parks, etc.

There are also mixed-use development buildings that are sometimes categorized as commercial properties in the real estate industry and they actually have a growth in demand. These kinds of properties usually have a mix of uses ranging from residential to retail and sometimes the public sector. For instance, a mixed-use property may have apartment units on the upper floors and maybe shopping centers on the lower floors.

Before getting started with commercial real estate, you should understand that is wide apart from residential real estate and so, even if you have been a residential real estate investor before, you must open your mind to learning and acquiring the best strategies for making commercial real estate work for you too. Next, let's look at investment opportunities in Commercial real estate.

INVESTMENT OPPORTUNITIES IN COMMERCIAL REAL ESTATE

There are two key investment opportunities in commercial real estate and these two are the only way an investor can make his income and get a return on investment. Firstly, real estate investment is distinct from traditional investment in a way: it holds value as a hard asset which means it has the capacity of being a source of income rather than being purchased for the potential selling value like most traditional investments e.g., bonds.

What this means is that you can always make money from your real estate investment even while waiting for the selling potential to increase and therein lies the investment opportunities in commercial real estate.

Commercial real estate investment has a simple and straightforward strategy: there is always an upsurge in demand for real estate in any particular area. So, investors purchase property in this area and then make their income through two ways: first, they lease the property to a commercial tenant who would like to use the property for business in exchange for rent; and second, they sell or resell the property after it has appreciated in value over the years. There you have the two investment opportunities commercial real estate presents to you. Let's look at them more closely.

Rental Income Investment

Each category of commercial real estate property that we have examined above has its tenants, which are typically different from the others. Unsurprisingly, each differing tenant also comes with different property management needs, lease agreements, and different arrangements. For instance, office properties as we have examined above are typically arranged with cubicles and parking decks. Furthermore, the lease agreement usually requires the tenant to pay the rent with a 5 to 10 years range in the lease terms. On the other hand, multifamily apartment properties expectedly have families and individuals as tenants with lease agreements that are typically either long term or short term. This may range month to month to as long as a year. Apartment buildings also have more tenants and leases to manage when compared to office properties.

Add Value or Appreciation

The second investment opportunity that brings a return on investment for commercial real estate investors is the increase in the value of a property over the period it was held by the investor. Of course, properties either add value or lose value depending on the strategy of the investor. Even the best of strategies can't guarantee gains to investors due to other economic variables which may arise and affect the market. But, when an investor takes the time to research the market and come up with a strategy using some of the tips you will be getting throughout the course of the book, value appreciation of investment properties will be guaranteed, mostly always.

In clearer terms, real estate is a scarce asset because of the inability to "create" more lands and this scarcity facilitates an increase in demand, which is what real estate investors capitalize on. When demand increases for a property you have previously bought, or in an area around the property, there is every chance you will have tenants willing to pay higher rents or potential buyers who will be willing to pay a higher price than you originally invested to purchase the property.

Time and demand, however, aren't the only factors that cause the value of a property to appreciate. Skilled and experienced investors also take matters into their own hands by using a "value-add" approach of making improvements to the property to add to its intrinsic value and upgrade its ability to earn more income. For instance, an investor may improve the cosmetic details of a multifamily property, thereby making it an attraction to individuals and families looking to rent an apartment. Then, he naturally charges higher rents. Investing money in renovating and upgrading a property will boost the potential selling price of this property in the future.

There are two methods of investing in commercial real estate: Direct investment and indirect investment.

Direct investment has to do with an investor acquiring direct ownership of a physical property i.e. becoming the landlord. This type of investment is more expensive and of course, requires more capital. Direct investment is not suitable for you if you don't already have extensive knowledge of the industry and market and you can't afford to pay people who do. CRE requires a large chump of capital for investment so you will, of course, be a high-net-worth individual to invest directly in the market. The model property is found in an area with low CRE supply and a significantly high demand, which will serve as basis for favorable rental prices. The local economy of the area will also affect the value of the CRE property.

Indirect investment involves investing in commercial real estate any acquiring ownership of different market securities like Exchange-traded funds, Real Estate investment Trusts and, investing in companies which naturally attend to the commercial real estate market e.g. banks.

HERE'S WHY YOU SHOULD INVEST IN COMMERCIAL REAL ESTATE: PROS AND CONS OF INVESTMENT

If you are wondering what the fuss about commercial real estate is and why you should bother investing in it, you probably don't know yet that commercial real estate offers both financial and personal rewards which will benefit you a lot. Some investors acquire commercial real estate properties solely for the purpose of building wealth and a steady source of income i.e. financial security. Other investors utilize CRE for portfolio diversification and tax benefits. You don't have to be either of these categories of investors because everything is achievable together when you invest in commercial real estate.

Here are some of the benefits you stand to gain from CRE;

- **Higher source of income**

Every commercial real estate investor who has gone about it the right way and has been successful at investment will tell you that CRE is a sure source of higher and steady income. In real estate generally, commercial properties have a higher return on investment (ROI) than residential real estate: CRE has an average of 6 to 12 percent ROI while single-family residential properties have an average of 1 to 4 percent. CRE properties also offer a lower vacancy risk since the properties tend to have more units. Plus, commercial real estate properties usually have longer lease terms, which eliminates the problem of having to deal with low tenant turnover.

- **Steady Cash Flow**

Another benefit of commercial real estate that is actually quite distinct to it is that: it provides a consistent stream of income thanks to the longer lease agreements. For instance, an office space that has been leased on a 5-years agreement will provide a real estate investor with a consistent source of income than a single-family building that the lease term is probably one year or below. In addition, CRE properties have more units than residential buildings, which means an investor can increase income streams quire faster. This is known in the CRE market as a triple net lease. Typical in CRE, tenants also pay the property's real estate taxes, insurance, maintenance costs, etc. thereby increasing the benefits the owner stand to gain.

- **Low Competition**

Most real estate investors and investors generally have a preconceived notion of commercial real estate investment as being seemingly difficult, making them unwilling to break into the territory. What this means for you as a commercial real estate investor is that: you have relatively low competition. Unlike the residential real estate investment where there is a saturation of investors, CRE provides you the advantage of lesser competition which naturally opens you to more opportunities and of course, gains.

- **Attractive Lease Terms**

A longer lease agreement is definitely one of the perks to enjoy as a commercial real estate investor. Commercial real estate properties come with attractive lease terms that provides the investors an opportunity to generate impressive returns on investment and a significant and consistent flow of cash. In most cases, CRE lease contracts are signed for a minimum of 3 years, which can extend for as many years as possible. This longer lease agreement also ensures less volatility in the market, and a consistent rental income, which potentially mitigates risks related to economic swings. Also, direct investments in CRE, as we have said above, has less volatility in comparison with traditional investments such as stocks and bonds. Since direct real estate investments aren't publicly traded, the market is rarely impacted by dynamic news and events, which mostly always affects traditional investment markets.

Apart from these, there are much more benefits which an investor may stand to gain in Commercial real estate investment. These benefits make commercial real estate a better investment market than residential real estate. But as with all things, CRE investment has its disadvantages as much as it has the advantages. What are the cons of investing in commercial real estate?

- **Considerable amount of Time investment**

Owning a commercial real estate property is quite different from owning a residential real estate because with commercial properties, you have a lot more than a single-family property to manage. CRE investment requires a lot of commitment in terms of time invested because there is no other way to ensure a return on investment. You simply can't be an absentee landlord sitting somewhere and waiting for your investment to maximize itself. As a commercial property investor, you will probably have to manage multiple leases, annual Common Area Maintenance (CAM), public safety concerns and other maintenance issues. If you are lucky enough to invest in more than a property, this, of course, means more management work for you. So, it's not advisable to invest in commercial real estate if you don't have the time to commit to it. CRE requires as much time investment as capital investment.

- **Professional Help**

An individual with the "I will do it all myself" mindset simply can't succeed when it comes to commercial real estate investment; it is impossible. Naturally, you will require the help of licensed professionals to help cater to some of the maintenance issues in a commercial property. Ranging from repairs to emergencies, it pays to have someone to help with some of the issues you will be dealing with. This, of course, means added cost for you. Although this added cost isn't quite ideal, you may need to include it in your set of expenses from the start so the property can be properly managed and taken care of. You should always remember to consider property management costs when evaluating the amount to use in purchasing a commercial investment property. Averagely, property management companies charge around 5 to 10 percent of rental revenue for management, including lease administration. The best thing is to strategically evaluate your position and understand whether you can manage the leasing and all yourself, or if it will be better to outsource the responsibilities to professionals.

- **Large Initial Investment**

Naturally, the cost of acquiring a commercial real estate property is larger than what it costs to acquire a residential property in the same local area. Therefore, commercial real estate requires a larger capital for investment. When you acquire a commercial property, you can typically expect some larger capital expenditure to follow suit. For instance, you may have already purchased a commercial property and a new expenditure comes in the form of repairs or renovations to certain areas of the property. Since commercial properties have more units and expectedly more tenants, it also means you have more facilities to maintain which of course translates into more costs for you. The only thing in CRE investment is that there is always a likely chance that the gain in revenue will outweigh the cost of investment in comparison to when you invest in a residential property.

- **Higher Risks**

This is not surprising as markets with larger ROI opportunitics as the CRE market typically present higher risks. It is a simple case of, "the larger the rewards, the higher the risks." If you are adverse to risks, commercial real estate isn't for you because anything can happen, at any time. Commercial properties are used for public purposes and as such, have more public visitors, which means more people come on the property every day. These people may get hurt or do something that damages the property. For examples, a car may hit a patron in the parking lot; a child may slip on ice in winter; and someone may decide to spray some part of the building with paints. Incidents like these are common to commercial properties and they happen everywhere.

To increase your knowledge of the risks involved in commercial real estate investment, let's take a further look at the kind of risks to expect.

WHAT ARE THE RISKS OF COMMERCIAL REAL ESTATE INVESTMENT?

No investment opportunity that offers so many benefits and advantages as CRE comes without risks. To invest in commercial real estate, you must have a solid risk tolerance level. Every investor has a different risk tolerance level. Some investors prefer to invest in high-risk, high-profit properties, while others lean towards lower risk properties. Therefore, you must know and prepare your mind as an investor for the potential risks CRE is likely to present you with. Understanding the risks involved in investing in commercial real estate will help you put up a good and successful fight when you do face these risks. So, let's examine the potential risks an investor is likely to experience in commercial real estate investment!

Economic Climate

Certain risks in commercial real estate are uncontrollable and one of these is the market and economic climate. These are extraneous factors which you have little or no control over as an investor.

Economic volatility, unemployment rate, inflation rate, and unexpected geopolitical events are such factors that impact the market climate and therefore affects commercial property investment. As an investor, you need to be up-to-date with news and details of local, national, and international events that could have an effect on the commercial real estate market. It is quite risky to try to make predictions about what may occur in the future and it is also dangerous since it makes CRE investors vulnerable to reacting to every news in the paper or on the TV. Rather, as an experienced investor, you will instead analytically examine how trends impact commercial real estate over time and then use this to make calculated and informed guessed on whether these variables will have a major impact in the market, based on the type of commercial property you own.

Unexpected Incidents

In commercial real estate, there are certain events that you simply can't predict or prevent because they are out of your hand. Some of these include natural disasters, man-made disasters, criminal threats, etc. which can occur at any time, without prior warning.

Dynamism of Competitive Environment

Changes occur in the commercial real estate market and these changes, of course, affect your investment. Technological development and changes in location needs are some of the changes that can impact the commercial real estate market.

For instance, the recent willingness of companies to allow their employees work to from home and in non-traditional office spaces has led to a decrease in the need for office spaces.

Other risks that a commercial real estate investor is likely to face include:

- Business risks: These are risks that impact the bottom line performance of a property. Examples are increased taxes, higher operating costs, and increased labor costs. Major risks include inflation, regulation changes, rising costs of purchase, and technological advancements, which may make a business or product go out-of-date.
- Interest rate risks
- Cash solvency risks
- Supply and demand
- Unstable market changes
- Management risks
- Financial regulatory reforms
- Tax code revisions etc.

How do you respond to risks in commercial real estate?

Most of the CRE risks that have been listed above are out of your control so the idea is to respond to critical risks only. Other risks usually have very little impact on your property or the investment goals you set so they can always be ignored.

Doing this will leave you with a minor subset of risks that will affect your business severely if not properly dealt with. These risks can cause permanent property damage, result in you to losing a whole lot of money, or result in property default. The key is to put a strategic set of procedures in place to always deal with these types of risks. Interestingly, some risks can actually present you with a golden opportunity which you can take advantage of to make you more money.

No matter the procedures you set in place for counter-responding to risks, however, you will always be affected by two critical factors which are; how well you do your due diligence and your ability to set aside emotions when making important decisions. As you read on, you will learn more about due diligence and how to do it the right way.

Chapter 2

* * * * * *

Guiding Principles: Everything You Need to Get Started with Commercial Real Estate

Becoming a successful commercial real estate investor opens you up to a lucrative career path, but if you don't start the right way, there is every chance that your commercial real estate venture may turn out unsuccessful. There are critical steps that a beginner like you will need to take when getting started in commercial real estate investment. Taking these steps will help maximize your potentials and increase the likelihood of success in investment.

As a beginner in the commercial real estate investment market, the first step to take is to set investment goals. Setting down realistic goals you want to achieve in commercial real estate is the pathway to achieving the results you want. When you set down specific goals with realistic deadlines, your mind becomes clearly defined and you become sure of where to start.

Next is to have an investment plan which you will follow in reaching your investment targets. In commercial real estate, you shouldn't just purchase any property. There are things to do before determining if a property is worth investing in or purchasing. A savvy investor creates an investment plan for property purchases so he or she can better get the returns and growths on investment they want. Every investment you make should put you ahead of the game. One thing to note is that the plan you create will always impact the investment strategy or approach you take towards commercial real estate investment.

After you have clearly drawn a plan to achieve your investment goals in commercial real estate, the next step to take is to decide on the best strategy to go about the plan you have clearly drawn. An investment strategy is imperative to your plan because it helps you understand the best ways to go about achieving your goals and reaching the milestones you have set. Sometimes, the type of property you are planning to purchase determines the kind of strategy you approach investment with. There are two typical commercial real estate investment strategy and they are:

- **Cash Flow strategy**

The cash flow strategy involves understanding and managing your investment expectations. What this implies is that as an investor, you should be able to analyze and understand what to expect when you purchase a particular property. When creating a cash flow strategy, you should always ask yourself two pertinent questions: First, if a property has a lower monthly cash flow, is it a good deal? Second, if a property has a higher monthly cash flow, does that make it a right addition or deal to my portfolio?

Answering these questions will help you decide the approach to take. Like we have said, each property will probably require a different strategy from the other. So, always note down your expectations and then without emotions or bias, determine if this property meets the expectations you have set down and if it will help you reach the financial milestones you set for yourself.

The idea behind using a cash flow strategy is that it is a more passive investment strategy that doesn't require a hands-on approach like the value-add strategy.

- **Value Add**

This is a more hands-on strategy that you can use with properties that typically require some form of renovations before you can lease it out or get a higher return on capital investment. These properties usually need renovation, have maintenance issues, or have structural issues that need to be improved on.

If your investment plan is to invest in only add value properties, the best strategy to have is naturally the add-value strategy. With this kind of strategy, you will need a local team with which you can complete every stage of the property. You will also need to put the potential appreciation value of the property into consideration.

Understanding how commercial real estate financing works is another thing you need before you start investing in commercial real estate. You should also keep track of your financial records so you can know if you really have the money to invest in commercial real estate. Investing in commercial properties require to have a higher net worth than residential real estate investment and you must be able to make the financial commitment. Keeping track of your total income will give you an insight into how much cash you can invest in a property. Having a small amount of cash available doesn't, however, translate to being unable to invest. There are other means of getting investment capitals for commercial real estate, which we will examine in a subsequent chapter.

If you have analyzed your finances and you realize you will need a loan to complement the cash you have ready for investment, you need to get a pre-approval for the loan. A pre-approval can be gotten through a trusted lender or mortgage broker. You can always consult a broker before applying for loan pre-approval if you are really unsure of your financial ability in investing in a commercial property.

Also, a successful investor always has his risk tolerance mapped out. To be that successful commercial real estate investor, make sure you have a risk profile that clearly lists out all of the risks you are willing to take for the business. Your attitude towards risks will highly impact your investment strategy and how successful it is.

Creating a budget is another step you must take so you can create a balance between your income and expenses, mostly positive. A budget not only lets you know where all your money is going, but it also makes it possible for you to expand your plan for potential bigger expenses.

Once you have everything you need to start in place and you are sure you really want to venture into an unchartered territory like the commercial real estate market, it is time to get yourself familiar with important technical terms in commercial real estate. Knowing and understanding what these terms mean will clearly set you apart from a commercial real estate beginner (which you are!).

TECHNICAL COMMERCIAL REAL ESTATE TERMS YOU SHOULD BECOME FAMILIAR WITH

Every industry has technical terms that are peculiar to it and a beginner can be clearly identified by his understanding and use of these terms. In order not to stand out as a commercial real estate beginner or amateur, it is necessary that you familiarize yourself with the most important commercial real estate terms which every CRE investor should know. Being able to understand basic terminologies will go a long way in getting you acclimated to the market and also ensure you are not cheated or played on while trying to land a deal. These are 10 of the key terms a commercial real estate investor should know;

- **Net Operating Income (Rental income – Expenses)**

This is one term every commercial real estate investor should understand because it will largely impact how successful you are with your real estate investments. Net operating income (NOI) is the heart of any commercial real estate deal and it refers to income generated annually from a property after all property expenses have been taken care of, excluding mortgage payment or depreciation.

Property expenses typically include any expenses that make it possible for you to run and maintain an investment property such as property management fees, utility, and property taxes. NOI doesn't include amortization, depreciation, loan payments, or capital expenditures and it is usually calculated before tax. The more the NOI increases, the higher the value of a property becomes and if NOI goes down, the value of a property also goes down. Note that you can also generate other incomes such as parking lot or laundry apart from rent on a commercial property.

- **Cash on Cash Return**

Usually calculated before taxes, cash on cash return is one of the most common terms in commercial real estate because it is in fact another word for the return on your investment. Cash on cash is the measure of your property's annual cash flow divided by your property's down payment.

- **Return on Investment**

Return on investment or ROI as most people prefer to call it is the calculated amount you get back from an investment property known as the return, divided by the cost of the property. In clearer terms, ROI is not how much you spend on an investment. Rather, it is how much you are able to get out of the property and how fast you are able to get it. ROI can be largely impacted by several variables such as renovation costs, maintenance costs, and the amount of loan you originally borrowed to invest in the property.

- **Capitalization Rate**

The capitalization rate or simply "cap rate" is gotten by dividing the Net operating income (NOI) by an income property's sale price or asking price. A cap rate is the heart of every calculation in commercial real estate because it helps you figure out your potential return on investment before considering other factors like potential mortgage financing. Usually, a lower cap rate means a higher price point, while higher cap rate means lesser risks. In beginners' term, the cap rate is the potential ROI if you pay for a property with all cash, no mortgage or loan.

- **Debt Coverage Ratio**

Also known as the debt service coverage ratio (DSCR), the debt coverage ratio (DCR) is used to compare the Net operating income of an investment property with its debt service. It is terminology that investors typically use with lenders and it used by lenders to calculate if you will be able to generate enough income to pay back your loan. A DCR of 1.15 to 1.35 multiplied by the NOI/annual debt service is usually required by lenders before they give you a loan.

- **Loan to Value**

As a beginner who is considering how to invest in commercial real estate, the Loan to Value (LTV) is something you will come across over and over. Your LTV is determined by the percentage of a property's value or sale price, which is attributed to financing.

Lenders assign a higher LTV to investment properties that have lower risk.

- **Building Classifications**

This is the terminology for asset classification, which most property values are determined by. Commercial real estate property fall under any of these 4 categories: Class A, Class B, Class C, and Class D. The market value of a property determines what category it falls under. Like we already analyzed in chapter one, Class A properties are those that are located in excellent areas, great aesthetics with major amenities and they naturally have a higher demand rate. You charge the highest rents for Class A properties. Investment properties which fall under Class B, C, or D are those that are less aesthetically appealing than Class A income properties. They are mostly based in locations that aren't quite desirable.

The higher the class of an income property, the higher in demand it is. One thing about the property classes is that Class A properties usually offer a lower return on investment while the lesser classes offer more ROI with greater risks since they are less appealing in the market. Another thing is that properties in lower classes require more renovations and maintenance. Commercial real estate beginners are advised to invest more in Classes B, C, and D properties since they provide a balance between risk and return. Make sure you become conversant with how to identify various asset classifications for when you have a purchase to make.

- **Price Per Unit**

The price per unit helps an investor determine the worth of a property and how much to pay for a purchase. For instance, if you have $100,000 and you want to purchase a property with 10 units, the price per unit would be $10,000, which you get by dividing the amount you have by the number of units in the building. That is simply your price per unit and it is at the heart of every commercial property you purchase. There is also the price per square footage that is used when calculating the cost of commercial properties like office buildings, retails, and industrials. Price per unit is usually used for apartment buildings. Understanding both price per unit and price per square footage will help you know if the price a seller is requesting for a property is realistic or not.

- **REIT**

This is a Real Estate Investment Trust that is used for a corporation that controls or finances investment properties. A REIT is similar to traditional investments like Stocks. It typically involves you buying shares in an investment property and receiving dividends on the rental income generated by the property management company controlling the property. There is a considerable return on investment on REITS for commercial real estate investors, which makes it an enticing choice of investment. However, REITS are accompanied by some level of risks due to the price volatility vulnerability. Owing to this, experienced investors prefer to diversify their investment portfolio by buying properties and mixing it up with REIT investments.

- **Lease**

A lease is a written legal agreement between a property owner i.e. you and the tenant. Leases are the lifeline of your commercial property and there are different types of leases. They include office, retail and apartments.

There you have them; the ten important commercial real estate tips that you should master as a potential investor so that you can stand apart from the amateurs and beginners. An apt understanding of the commercial real estate terminologies will massively impact your rise to the top in the commercial real estate investment market. They will serve as major boosts to your investment relationships, negotiations, and also give you the confidence you need to discuss prospects with sellers and buyers alike!

Chapter 3

The Secrets to Evaluating Commercial Real Estate Investment Property

Evaluating commercial real estate investment property means determining the worth or value of a property. There are many approaches to unraveling a property's worth, but we will examine the three most common and direct approaches. Evaluating an asset also requires that you understand certain important metrics. These metrics are what you break down to figure out the value of a property.

The first approach to evaluating commercial property is the **Income Approach.** This approach is the most commonly used method of appraising the value of a property. The income approach is used to estimate a property's value by calculating how much the property is expected to generate in the future. To calculate the value of an asset using the income approach, you need to understand the NOI and Cap rate, which we have already discussed previously. Remember we said that NOI is the Net operating income i.e. the income generated from an investment after all property expenses have been subtracted while the cap rate is the ratio of the NOI to a property's value. In other words, NOI = Gross income – operating expenses while Cap Rate = NOI / Value.

To use the income approach for evaluating property value, you must have already created a pro-forma that shows the expected NOI. Then, you add a cap rate to the equation. The pro of this approach is that it allows you to determine what you are willing to pay for a property. However, it also has its con, which is that each investor has varying tolerance for cap rates.

Income approach is one of the most accurate methods of appraising property value. However, extra work must be put into ensuring that the Net operating income is accurate because miscalculating or underestimating vacancy rate can result in skewed results and numbers.

The GRM approach is one of the easiest methods of evaluating commercial real estate property and it is a popular approach used by real estate investors. Although similar to the income approach, the GRM value appraisal method is different because it uses a cap rate based on gross rental income rather than net operating income, which the Income approach uses. The GRM Multiplier is a number usually higher than one, while the income approach's cap rate is a percentage below 1. When an investor uses the gross rent multiplier method to evaluate a property; vacancy rates, repairs, collection loss, and expenses are not taken into consideration. GRM: Property value= GRM x Annual gross rents.

To accurately evaluate a property with the GRM, you need to know the GRM of similar properties around. This information is usually available with appraisers and real estate brokers. Most investors appreciate this method because of the simplicity. But like all things, it has its con which is the absence of vacancy rates, collection loss, and expenses; plus it is always difficult to access comparable properties and their GRMs.

The third approach to appraising property value, which you should know is the **Cost Approach.** This involves calculating the cost of rebuilding a property from scratch. Calculation typically includes the current cost of land, labor costs, cost of construction materials, and everything related to replacing the existing structure of the commercial property. In other words, this approach estimates that the value of a commercial property is equal to the cost you incurred in reconstructing it. The formula for calculating the cost approach is Property value = land value + (cost of rebuilding + accumulated depreciation).

The idea behind this approach is that buyers are expected not to spend more on a commercial property than they would spend on acquiring land and building a similar property from scratch. To calculate how much it costs to build a property from scratch, you can use any of the following methods.

- **Comparative unit method:** Investor calculates an estimate for the costs to rebuild property on a per square foot basis while considering various categories of construction materials.

- **Segregated cost method:** involves calculating the individual costs of different building components e.g. the cost of buying a new roof.

- **Unit-in-place method:** This is an advanced segregated cost method which further breaks down building components.

- **Quantity survey method:** Considered the most accurate form of new building cost calculation, this method has to do with creating a detailed estimate for every building component and material right to the exact quantity required to replace the existing structure, and the calculates the cost of labor accordingly.

These are the different approaches a commercial real estate investor can take in appraising the market value of an investment property so he or she can decide whether the property is worth investing in or not.

FACTORS THAT DETERMINE A PROPERTY'S VALUE

Several factors affect the property value of an asset and you must always take these properties into consideration when choosing a property for purchase. There are four important factors that can be used in estimating the value of a commercial property. But, apart from these four, there are some other factors. Not to worry, we will check out each of these factors so you can understand how it affects your choice of investment property.

Location of Property

The market area of a property is one of the foremost factors that affect a property's value and ultimately impact your investment. Properties that are located in central parts of the city that are excellently developed with easy transportation access have more market value than those which are located farther away from the center of the city and harder to reach. Commercial tenants want to be located in an area where employees, customers and suppliers can easily access therefore they would be willing to pay more to get a space in a building located in an area like that. Another reason why location impacts commercial real estate value is that tenants want to be positioned in a place where there is a higher chance of prospective customers passing regularly since prospects have a high likelihood of becoming real customers if the building is in a path where they frequently pass. The key is to scout out buildings that are located in an area where it seems like commercial real estate property is in demand.

- **Rental Income Potential**

The potential rental income is another major factor that impacts the value of commercial real estate property, and it is in turn, impacted by the location of the value or the aesthetic appeal the building has. If a building is located in an ideally developed area, it is bound to attract more tenants, which increases the market value of the property and opens way for the property owner to have potentially higher rental income. Also, the more spaces a commercial property has for rental, the higher the value becomes since the owner will naturally have more tenants to generate income from. A property's ability to yield more money for the owner increases the market value and the price of the property.

- **Number of Competitive Properties**

A major influence on the value of commercial real estate property is the competitive environment. This simply translates to the available number of properties that are similar in size, units, state, and income potential. Naturally, if an area has plenty of comparable properties, the value of properties in the same class lowers. In the same breath, if a property has features that stand out such as bigger spaces or better location than most of the similar properties around the area, the property's value becomes much more than it would have been if there were competitions. This is because the property would typically be more attractive to tenants than others. Even if a property is well located, if it is in an area with many comparable properties, the value of this property naturally falls. Therefore, you should always put comparable properties in consideration when valuing a property.

- **Interest Rates**

Interest rates have significant impact on the real estate market. When buying a commercial property with loans, you should ensure you research and calculate the interest rate first with a mortgage calculator. Changes in interest rate affect the investors' ability to purchase commercial property because the lower the interest rate, the lower the cost of obtaining a loan to purchase the property. This facilitates a higher demand of commercial property, thereby causing the prices to rise once again. Note that the more the interest rates rise, the more the cost of obtaining an investment loan increases.

- **Economic Changes**

The economy/economic changes are another factor that affects the value of commercial real estate property. The overall health of an economy can be a major determinant in the worth of the property. How the economy affects a property's value is usually measured with important economic indicators such as the employment data, unemployment rate, GDP, prices of products, manufacturing activity, etc. To be concise, when the economy lags, commercial real estate and real estate generally lags too. In fact, the economy affects every industry in the market so it isn't just a real estate thing.

One thing you should keep to mind, however, is that the changes in the economy will have different effects on different commercial real estate property types. For instance, if your investment is in special purposes property such as a hotel or a tourist resort, you will be more affected by an economic downturn than if you had invested in office or retail buildings. This is because hotels and tourists resorts are more directly impacted by sensitive economic activities due to the type of lease structure they typically acquire. For example, a downturn in the economy can turn customers away from hotels since it is a kind of short-term lease. On the other hand, tenant in office buildings or retails have longer lease agreements which can rarely be affected an economic downturn. Therefore, the type of commercial real estate you invest in will largely determine how affected you are by economic cyclicality.

Demographics

These are the date that defines the composition of a population and it includes race, age, gender, income class, population growth, and migration patterns. Demographics are often overlooked by many investors, but they do have significant effects on the value of real estate and the type of properties that are more in demand. A major shift in the demographics of a country can affect commercial real estate trends for as long as decades.

There are different ways by which a shift in demographics can affect the commercial real estate market. So, as an investor in multi-family properties, you should be able to ask some vital questions such as: i) How would the shift impact the demand for multi-family properties in popular areas? ii) How does it affect consumers' demand for larger homes if incomes become smaller and there are no longer children in the home? These questions and many others like them would help you narrow down the type of potentially attractive properties and their possible locations long before the trend even starts in the market. That makes you a savvy investor.

- **Government Policies, Subsidies, and Regulations**

These are extraneous factors out of your control and they also have considerable impact on the value of a commercial property. Government policies have an impact on the demand for property and the price of the property. Tax credits, subsidies, and deductions are some of the many ways the government can boost demand for commercial real estate temporarily as long as they stay put in place. A savvy investor, which is what you will be, is always ahead of himself in staying current on government policies and incentives so as to be able to determine a change in supply or demand and also recognize possibly fake trends. You should always recognize which factor is impacting the market and increasing or decreasing the value of commercial properties.

The commercial real estate market is a highly attractive and lucrative market for real estate investors due to the size and scale. Whether you are investing in a property through direct or indirect investment, you should always be aware of factors that can affect a property you are investing in.

Every factor that we have examined are high-level factors that have significant impacts on the commercial real estate market, but there are of course more complex parts that come to play in the overall movement of the CRE market. Some of these factors may indicate a clear-cut relationship between the market and the factors that move it, but in reality, they can achieve very different results. This doesn't rule out the importance of understanding these factors, however. Understanding the major factors that drive the commercial real estate market value is vital to an investor's ability to perform a thorough and comprehensive evaluation of a potential commercial investment property.

In the next chapter, you will be learning how to find great commercial real estate deals and how to evaluate them to make sure they are the right deals for you! The secret to finding great deals and understanding how to make them work for you lies in your understanding of the property appraisal methods and all the factors we just thoroughly examined. This is because you need this knowledge to navigate your way around finding a deal. So, ensure you understand this chapter very well before proceeding to the next!

Chapter 4

───── ❖──❖──❖ ─────

Find Great Commercial Deals:
What You Should Know

The ability to sniff out great commercial properties is crucial to survival in the commercial real estate market. As an investor, it will be a waste of precious resources if you are unable to effectively identify and seek out great real estate deals. In fact, this is something that could result in the loss of both investment capital and the return you anticipate on a deal. Finding great deals is not an easy thing to achieve. Even when you are an experienced commercial real estate investor, there are cases where you just land some really bad deals that could make you lose money. In order to find the best deals, hard work and market experience are two important factors that have a big part to play.

The key to any good commercial real estate investment is to find an undervalued property that has a pretty good investment opportunity. To be factual, if finding good deals in the commercial real estate market was an easy thing to do, a lot of people would be in the industry investing in different properties. However, one thing about commercial real estate is that hard work mostly always pays off. Once an investor puts in the required amount of work and is able to find a great commercial deal, there is always the potential to make huge returns on the investment.

There are many factors that come to play when you are trying to determine what the right deal is. For example, location is a critical determinant of a property's value and you can always evaluate how ideal it is to invest in a commercial real estate property by considering the location. Commercial properties have the potential of appreciating greatly in value if an investor gets the right location. However, there are also other things you must consider when looking for the right commercial real estate deal for you. Here is one thing to take away; it is always easier and recommended to work hand-in-hand with a trusted and experienced broker when finding commercial properties, especially as someone new to the commercial real estate market. Brokers work together with investors to locate a great deal and sealing it at the right price that ensures maximum return on investment.

Time is the number one thing you must always put in mind when fishing for good deals in the commercial market. Every savvy commercial real estate investor knows that time is always the essence in the industry, especially when you are trying to score a deal. You aren't the only investor in the market so you should know that there are always people out there looking for the same deals as you. Therefore, time is utmost importance so you can always beat competitors to a good deal. If you take time to be of trivial use in the industry, then there will always be someone in the market to hijack your great deal. There is one thing most seasoned commercial real estate investors wish they had someone to tell them right from when they ventured into the industry and it is that, "The highest offer isn't always the accepted offer; the first offer is." What this means is that once you are late to the party, there is the possibility that you may not be able to get that coveted property anymore. Many times, sellers will prefer to sell a property to the person that came with the first offer not considering whether the offers that come after are much higher. So, you should always keep this in mind to avoid losing out on valuable deals when seeking out the best commercial properties.

Numbers, numbers, numbers. It can't be stressed enough that commercial real estate is a game of numbers and you must be ready to play if you really want to find those great deals. The more the number of properties you go out to look at, the higher your chances of finding very lucrative deals. Again, this is why you require the help of an experienced broker because you simply won't be able to go out and look for properties in different locations all by yourself. Some brokers often offer real estate databases where you can scan through commercial properties for sale. Never be comfortable with checking out one or two properties when looking for awesome deals. Sometimes, you may not even get a potentially lucrative commercial property until you have checked a number of properties. Also, the more the number of commercial properties you are able to discover for potential purchase, the better your chances of finding more than one property with very high return on investment.

Value is another important thing to keep in mind when fishing for commercial real estate deals. As an investor, one thing you have to learn early in your career is that commercial properties aren't created equal. A successful investor is one who has effectively mastered the art of appraising and evaluating a property's worth accurately and this is what you should aspire to be. Knowing how to evaluate a property accurately opens your eye to numbers that reflect a commercial property's value and these numbers always play a great part when you are negotiating and trying to land a deal with a seller. A property's value is something that determines whether you have a great deal or not. Like we have said, a property's value is influenced by location, rental income potential, interest rate, number of competitive properties, etc. Another thing to note is that some properties have good market value but, when the cost and operating income outweigh, they usually spoil a deal which otherwise would have been great for you. In another chapter, you will learn everything you need to accurately evaluate a property so you can be a successful commercial real estate investor.

based on the numbers!   *this one hold*
                             this one flip

An **exit strategy** is also an essential marker of finding good deals. A savvy investor always recognizes a property with great prospects when he or she walks into the deal with exit strategy options in mind. You should always open your eye to land damage, areas of risk, potential repairs, and other important things when determining whether a property would be rehabilitated, wholesaled, or buy and hold. For instance, when you find a good deal that you feel isn't suitable for you but meets the qualifications of another investor in your network who is on the lookout for a deal, it is advisable to

is it a value Add property   *cap rate*   *Know the market,*
                                                            to decide.
Acquisition, Operating, Disposition of Asset, class.
DSCR 1.25+ cost.   *1) cash out refi u hold*
does f property   *OR*
area is important.   *2) buy o flip*

43

wholesale the property. Then, if you get a deal in a rentable market with a property in relatively good condition, buying and holding would be the best way to go for that particular property.

Motivation is the last most important thing you need for landing good investment deals but this isn't necessarily about you, although it is important that you are motivated about any deal you are trying to secure. However, what is most important is that you should always make sure you are securing deals with **motivated sellers.** This is key to your success in the commercial real estate industry. An investor always looks for sellers with motivation because they are sometimes willing to accept a very low price for a property and a cheap deal is something any investor should always look for. The cheapest deals often come with very low prices when the seller really needs to sell i.e. they have a very high motivation level. It could be that the seller is moving to a new place or he or she can no longer make payments on the property. To find motivated sellers is as easy as adding 1 plus 1 if you are willing to take a few steps. Firstly, you need to purchase a list e.g. a tax delinquent list. Once you have the list, take your time to get the contacts information including email addresses one way or the other. With the email addresses, you can use direct mail marketing to contact sellers who you feel are very motivated. The thing about direct mail marketing is that it is mostly effective since you are targeting a specific audience that may have actually been looking for the kind of information you are sending.

Finally, you should be savvy with finding deals **online** because that is another place where you can secure some really good deals. Taking advantage of technology can go a really long way in helping you find and seal good deals. Get online and find marketplaces that are made specifically for commercial real estate buyers and sellers. For instance, there is a private market place called Brevitas and you can secure very good deals here right from finding the right property to signing the agreement, all from the comfort of your computer. You don't even need to go on a physical lookout for properties. However, it is best for you to combine online and physical search for valuable properties rather than just stick to one method. Brokers naturally have an idea of the different ways you can search for good commercial properties for sale online so again, make sure you work with a trusted broker to make your work easy and successful.

Next is how you can accurately evaluate commercial real estate deals to ensure that it is indeed a good deal for you with a high ROI.

EVALUATING COMMERCIAL REAL ESTATE DEALS

Before you go ahead to sign a contract on any deal, it is crucial that you evaluate the deal so you can determine if it is the right deal to invest in or not. Evaluating a commercial real estate deal is no easy thing to do but once you know the right way to go about it, you will find it to be straightforward. When it comes to evaluating a property, you must be someone who is able to put great attention to details while considering both tangible and intangible factors that we have already discussed in a previous chapter. By appraising a property and assessing the potential revenue and cost for the first year of purchase, you can easily determine the profitability of investing in the property. Evaluating a property comes in four stages, which we will be looking at one by one, with examples.

1. Calculate the property's income, price, and value

Firstly, get an estimate of the Gross Scheduled Income (GSI). Do this by adding up the total rent which can be expected to come from renting out the commercial property. Ensure that the potential rent of each area of space is tailored according to the market value of the property. You can do this with Apartment complexes, office buildings, and strip malls. For instance, a 3-bedroom apartment will naturally rent out for more than a 2-bedroom apartment space in the same complex. So, the GSI should be estimated according to the size of each area of space.

Once you have the estimated GSI, the next thing is to subtract a 5% vacancy. This is because not all unit of space in commercial property will stay rented through a full year. So, you must make sure to consider this in your calculations by subtracting a 5% vacancy from the GSI. The number you get after doing this is referred to as the effective gross income (EGI) and this is what lenders will use when assessing your potential purchase.

After this, you need to calculate the Net Operating Income, which we have already said is the heart of any commercial deal. The NOI is vital because it helps you ascertain whether the property is one you will profit from or not. To calculate the Net Operating Income, determine the property's first year estimated gross operating income. Then, determine the expected operating expenses for the same period of time. Now, subtract the estimated expenses from the estimated income. The number you get is your NOI and if it is positive, it means the property will yield initial profit. For your calculations to be even more accurate, you could consider replacing the Gross Estimated Income with the Effective Gross Income in your calculations.

Now, calculate the capitalization rate or "Cap rate", which we have also discussed in an early chapter. The cap rate is gotten by dividing the net operating income i.e. NOI with the price of the property. Doing this will give you a percentage which is your cap rate. The cap rate is usually influenced by the area and the real estate offerings. With the capitalization, you are able to tell your potential profit margin from a commercial property.

Next, go ahead and divide the NOI by the cap rate to get an ideal price for the property you want to purchase. Whether you are buying or selling a property, you must always come up with a sales price that suits the market. Dividing your potential NOI by the cap rate for the area where you are purchasing a property will give you a sales price that includes your profits and operating expenses. After doing this, calculate the GRM i.e. gross rental multiplier which you can use to determine profitability. Get a copy of the listed selling price for the space and divide it by the annual gross rental income to get the GRM. You should also do your calculations with many properties so you can average the results for a market area. Lastly, use your Gross Rental Multiplier to ascertain a property value estimate. To do this, multiply the annual gross rents of the commercial property or the market area by the GRM. The resulting number is the market value estimate based on the current market.

Here is an example to help you understand better;

- Let us assume that your **GSI** for a property is **$100,000.**
- Subtracting **5%** from the GSI will give you **$90,000.**
- With estimated **operating expenses** of **$50,000** subtracted from your GSI which is **$100,000**, you will get an **NOI** of **$50, 000.** If subtracted from the **EGI**, the NOI will be **$40,000.**
- If the price of the property is valued at maybe $**200,000** and the NOI is **$40,000**, you will get a cap rate of **20 percent**.
- To determine an ideal price for the property, divide the **NOI** by **cap rate** to get an ideal price of **$200, 000**.
- If the property's sales price is $250,000 and the annual gross rents is $20,000, you will have a **GRM** that is **12.5.**
- With the annual gross rent of $20,000 and a GRM of 12.5, a reasonable property value estimate will be **$250,000.**

There, you have successfully evaluated the worth of the property. The second stage is to consider important financial factors.

2. Weigh important financial factors

One of the main differences between commercial real estate and residential real estate is the calculation of square footage in determining the value of a property. To properly evaluate a property, you should ensure to check through the appraisals and documentation provided by the seller so as to verify if the seller listed the complete square footage for the building or property. If the square footage differs even slightly, ensure you address this with the seller in the early part of the negotiations. Keep it in mind that the value of any commercial property is directly linked to the square footage available for use in the property. Calculate your price per square footage (PPSF) by dividing the property's sales price by the total square footage.

If a property has areas that need repairs, it should factor in when you are evaluating the value of such property. Always look meticulously for damaged areas requiring repairs. Considering this aspect, it is vital to work together with a professional commercial property inspector who is experienced at sniffing out possibly damaged areas. If a property has areas that need touch and repair before it can be rented or leased out, you should deduct the cost of repairs from the potential revenue. Inability to properly inspect a property before purchase will result in costs that weren't part of your budget and this will end up affecting your profits. For this, you should endeavor to inspect any property in person if you can't get a professional inspector. It is also necessary for you to calculate the possible cost of repairs over time. Inquire about the condition and age of plumbing, electrical, and other important mechanical aspects of the commercial property. Then, compare the current age of the items with the total number of usage so you can have an idea of what you will need to repair or fix in both the short and long term. For instance, if the plumbing in the property is around 20 years old, then you know it may be needing repairs or replacement any time which means the possible cost of the replacement/repair should factor into your calculation of cost of repairs.

Asking the seller for the current owner's income and expenses paperwork is something you should also do once you are firm in your interest in the property. Once you have expressed a firm interest in the deal, the seller or their representative should be willing to give you paperwork of the previous year's occupation. You may also request for the tax documents, revenue documentations, and electricity bills. Also, make sure you go over the Annual Property Operating Data (APOD) report. This usually contains vital information about the rental income, loan details, operating expenses, and cash movements for a commercial property. The APOD report provides a complete financial image of a property over the previous year and you can always use it to ascertain future potential of the said property. Know that financial factors are an important aspect of accurately evaluating a property's worth.

3. Recognize the possible uses for the property

It is advisable and of utmost importance that you collaborate with financial specialists when evaluating a commercial real estate deal. Even if you are already an experienced commercial property investor, you should have an expert real estate team you work with. The most important people to have in your team are an accountant, a lawyer, and a trusted broker. The accountant will work to help you get a property without going out of budget; the lawyer will help with the negotiation process and the contract development and; the broker will work with you to find properties with huge return potentials. If you already have a broker, they can help you get a competent lawyer and accountant to work with.

To identify the possible uses for a commercial property, you will need information on the building's zoning laws and building codes. The zoning laws will help establish the type of businesses that can occupy the property and it may also limit the possible uses for the property. The building codes will provide information on the changes you are allowed to make to the building. This is particularly important if you are purchasing property in an area recognized for its history i.e. a place of historical importance.

Also, find out if the property is one that is fit for triple net leases. This is a term used when you rent out a property's space fully to renters who pay for the space's expenses directly on their own which means the only expenses you will have to pay as the owner is the overall mortgage for the building. Due to this, a property that meets the triple net lease criteria poses less of a financial risk. Ensure you also calculate the number of living quarters for apartment space. If you plan to use a property for multi-family housing, the revenue generated will be directly proportionate to the number of residents in the property. Appraise the layout of the building to figure out how it can be broken down into livable spaces. Put it in mind majority of multi-family commercial structures come with spaces for varying number of residents. For instance, an apartment complex typically comes with one, two, and three-bedroom rental options.

The uses for a commercial property factor in importantly when you are trying to estimate the true value of the property. So, ensure you put this duly into consideration when you are determining a property's value.

4. Factor in the intangible factors

The intangible factors that should be put in consideration when evaluating a commercial real estate deal are the seller's motivation level, area's development, crime rate, location of the property in the area, and other important factors. A seller's motivation level is an intangible factor that could affect the deal. Naturally, sellers who need to off-load a property quickly are always willing to sell at the lowest price while buyers with time will usually set the initial price very high.

It is also important to walk the neighborhood and have conversations with the residents to ascertain the area's development and crime rate. Also, find out about the vacancy level because renters would be unwilling to rent property in an area with plenty of vacancies. Consider any other potential residential issue you can identify too. Another thing is the position of the property in the area. Consider properties with the publicity value a storefront offers. If you are renting out the property space to businesses, then how the property appears on the outside is something you should make a big deal about. Determine if it is a high-traffic location that can provide significant exposure to the public and if there are similar businesses around the area.

Once you cover all four stages of evaluation meticulously, you will be able to tell the true value of a property and determine your potential return on investment.

CREATING A VALUABLE NETWORK

Creating a vast commercial real estate network is an essential action every investor who aspires to be successful must take. A network is one of the tools you need in the industry if you really want to make it big. Having a team of talents delegated to the right areas can present an investor with professional guidance, support, mutually beneficial partnerships, valuable experiences, and golden business relationships that could go a long way in determining his or her success in the commercial real estate industry. Naturally, as an entrepreneur, you need an effective network no matter the industry you are in.

Building up an effective, vast, and professional real estate network, however, goes beyond just exchanging business cards and cozying up to other investors, prospects, and real estate savvy people during happy hour. To create a successful network in the commercial real estate market, you need to be active, persuasive, and know how to communicate seamlessly with other people; this is something you may need a considerable amount of time and effort to learn. Not to worry though, we have simplified some of the best tips for building a professional real estate network to make the work easy for you.

A network is vital because it helps in building a database of prospects and in generating business referrals. In fact, some of your best deals may turn out to be from referrals or from other investors and commercial real estate-inclined people whom you have in your network. The first key to successfully create a network of professionals is to understand the importance of having a network; if you don't understand it, you cannot appreciate it. Networking provides you with an array of benefits which range from friendships and potential business relationships to investment leads. Once you are able to understand the benefits of having a reliable network presents to you, it becomes easier to appreciate how crucial it is to your success in the business. As a beginner in commercial real estate investment, some of the benefits you stand to gain from having a solid real estate network include;

- **Strong, valuable relationships**

Regularly assisting and engaging contacts in achieving their investment goals can be the foundation of very good relationships with other investors and it will, in fact, strengthen it the more. This could help form a bond and trust that will always be reciprocated over time, especially when you really need the help of a contact. The whole idea of networking is so investors can share critical and valuable information so as a newbie to the industry, the first thing you should do is to concentrate on building strong and valuable relationships which will definitely pay when the time is right.

- **Innovative ideas**

A quality and reliable real estate network can serve as a source of inspiration for bright, innovative ideas and perspectives that can shape your investment goals and objectives in the right way. Building relationships with people who are of like minds with you can give you access to information and insights from professionals who have been in the game before you. From such people, you can learn about the challenges, experiences, and hurdles which you are likely to come across in your stay in the commercial real estate market and you will probably also learn how you can deal with and overcome possible challenges in your own business.

- **Great reputation**

With the right commercial real estate network, you can build a good and reputable business to become a big brand in the industry. Quality real estate networks usually help new investors promote their status as industry experts so that they become reputable in the commercial community. When you attend important industry events regularly while helping other investors achieve certain goals, you will generate attention among investors and also boost your reputation as a savvy commercial real estate professional who is ever-willing to share his or her extensive knowledge about the commercial market. This also means building yourself up for when you would need other's help.

- **Opportunities and career advancement**

Another benefit you stand to gain from having a solid network is that you become open to many opportunities that other investors may not be able to access and these opportunities can go a long way in advancing your career. Networking presents you with opportunities for personal growth, career advancement, and business growth. In fact, it also becomes easier to meet prospects because there would always be people willing to introduce you to relevant industry players with potential referrals in the loom. Your network only expands more when you make it a priority.

- **Support**

The last but not least benefit of commercial real estate networks is the support you will be getting from more experienced people in the industry. Guidance and support from industry experts is an invaluable opportunity that networking provides you with.

Having looked at the benefits of creating a commercial real estate network, how do you build up your network by meeting relevant people and using contacts? Where can you meet these relevant people? One important thing to note is that anybody you meet could be a buyer or seller or a referral source that can be of help to you. Therefore, as an investor, you must erase all traits of being shy. A person looking to create a network must not be shy because he or she may just meet contacts anywhere. You must be ready to propel yourself beyond the confines of your comfort zone when needed. To create an amazing network and relationship with other investors and real estate experts in your area. Here are some of the best strategic places and events to attend.

- **Go to Property Auctions**

Auctions are something aspiring and beginner investor should always make efforts to attend because this is one of the best places where you can meet very serious-minded buyers and investors. Typically, auctions always require the winning bidder to close the purchase in a very short period of time, therefore, any buyer you meet here will be a serious one who is always ready to snag deals up. Go to auctions with the mindset of meeting as many people as possible and snatching up a lot of contacts you can build business relationships with. This is especially important if your plan is to purchase and sell commercial properties instead of renting them out. The people you meet at the auctions you go will be the ideal individuals to have on your buyers' database because they are ready to close deals quickly. Some companies also hold private auctions in specific cities around the country, so find out which you can attend. Here is an important tip to keep in mind: always be upfront with your new contacts when you meet them. Ensure you let them know what you do and also be straightforward enough to tell them you are on the lookout for new deals in the area. Someone who knows something about some property may end up being a source of referral to you!

- **Join Chamber of Commerce Groups**

Depending on the city you live, there are several networking groups collaborating together every month. They are often referred to as

Chamber of commerce groups and they usually occur in many major cities. Joining a chamber of commerce groups is a good and effective way of meeting professionals across different fields such as accounting, finance, and law. These people may turn out to be very helpful in some technical issues. Usually, these groups hold regular events such as networking breakfasts, luncheons, expos, and happy hours which you can take advantage of to make important business friends. You can meet buyers and more importantly, lenders who could fund your real estate transactions for you. One thing to remember is that you will be meeting a general audience since the chamber of commerce group isn't specific to your niche. Due to this, focus mainly on meeting local business owners and independent professionals who are willing to give and trade referrals and also, anybody else who you think might be helpful in the achievement of your commercial real estate goals and objectives.

- **Go to REIA and Landlord Meetings**

REIA meetings refers to Real Estate Investor Association where you can meet other investors like you while Landlord meeting is where you could meet property owners who may be looking to sell a property. These two meetings are great places for networking with other real estate professionals and professionals in the local industry. As a new investor, you should endeavor to attend these meeting as often as you can; making sure to network effectively and put your name out there in the market. At these meetings, you will be privileged to meet professionals of varying experience levels whom you can learn helpful tips and all from. However, keep in mind that not every city has a local REIA group. If your city is one of those without a group, you can even be the one to start a group. When attending these meetings, make it a priority to establish a conversation with some of the more experienced investors. Ask them about their business and the type of properties they prefer to deal with. This will enable you to build a rapport that could manifest into a beneficial business relationship with them.

- **Attend Home and Trade Shows**

Every year, tons of home and trade shows which you can take advantage of are held around the country. These events are usually some of the best sources of insights into industry trends and the reason behind these trends and you will surely meet hundreds of attendees from across the country ranging from contractors and lenders to suppliers. When you go to a trade show or home show, consider getting a booth, since hundreds or even thousands of people will come to the show over the course of a few days. Always attend a trade or home show with a specific strategy in mind so as to maximize your time and effort. Know what you want to achieve by attending the event and have a good strategy in place to help you accomplish your objective.

- **Explore Social Media**

In this new age, you cannot underestimate the influence of social media, especially social networking sites like Twitter, Facebook, and LinkedIn, which were built specifically for networking. These sites generate billion of viewers on a monthly basis and you can take advantage of that to create your commercial real estate investment network. The built-in audience may especially be of benefit to you as a new investor in the industry. Using hashtags and other features, you can connect with a range of individuals interested in the same things as you. To get the best of these social networking sites, think like a customer rather than a marketer. The key to maximizing the use of social media is to be "social." So, ensure you put in efforts to engage with users and be as likable as possible.

Important tips for Going to Events and Association Meetings

Firstly, always read and prepare ahead of time whether you are going for an auction, chamber of commerce group meeting, a trade show or anything else. This is to ensure you have an idea of what you will be discussing with the people you meet at the auction. Take your time to do a bit of research and be sure to come up with questions pertaining to the real estate industry. It is not compulsory that you have expert knowledge about these topics, but you should be able to hold a conversation on them. Since you are trying to create relationships, it doesn't make sense for you to just listen while the other person talks; it should be a two-way conversation. Credibility is also important in your conversations. Ensure you don't hide the fact that you are a beginner but also arm yourself with important commercial real estate knowledge before you go to any event. This will help the other professionals give you the respect you deserve, whether you are new to the market or not. Any question you ask should be related to real estate and more importantly, the conversation. Once you know enough to ask relevant questions, it means you have enough knowledge to participate in relevant real estate conversations. Many people advise new investors to "fake it till you make it," and while this may not necessarily be a bad thing, it's not a very admirable thing to do. Rather than fake your knowledge of the industry, be confident of the little you know while making conscious efforts to improve in the little you know. Never talk about things you have little or no knowledge about. If people find out you know less than you brag about, it will be a turn-off, which could seriously affect your goals of building a credible and efficient commercial real estate network.

Another tip is to always seek out people with common interests and goals. Commercial real estate investment is a great industry because of the many investment options open to you. But, one tricky thing about the industry is that there is a wholesome amount of information in the market, and most of this information may not even be relevant to your business. Therefore, you should aspire to get relevant information by seeking people with common interests only. For instance, if you are looking for means of financing your transaction and you happen to go to a chamber of commerce meeting, you should be actively looking out for professional lenders and accountants who may be willing to help you rather than talking to maybe a lawyer or contractor. The most efficient way of meeting people with common goals is to network with different people in different settings.

If you are able to get your first contact at a meeting or auction, never dismiss the connection. Put it in mind that it takes just a single person to revamp your life and business completely. This contact may go on to become a mentor, investment partner, or someone who gives you a referral on what may turn out to be your biggest investment deal. When you meet anybody, ensure you show a level of interest and curiosity about them and what they have to offer.

Even when you meet someone who doesn't seem to have common goals with you, never completely rule out that connection because you never know from whom you could get help and assistance. This person may know someone else who could be of immense assistance to your career.

As an aspiring commercial real estate investor, the most important factor that will singlehandedly affect your network building efforts positively or negatively (depending on you) is *Communication.* Your ability to effectively communicate with professionals and experts you meet while simultaneously cultivating a relationship will be of assistance in your short and long-term success. Creating a network may not be easy, but it is crucial to your success and is something you can achieve.

TOP MISTAKES TO AVOID AS A COMMERCIAL REAL ESTATE INVESTOR

As there are many opportunities for investors in the commercial real estate market, there are just as many mistakes that an investor could make if not very careful. Before you buy your first commercial property, it is vital that you know these mistakes beforehand so as to avoid making them.

1. Overanalyzing every detail of a deal

It is okay to want to get all the information you can on a deal, but what isn't okay is trying to get every minute piece of information to overanalyze the deal. Many investors think the more the information they have on a property, the better their purchasing decision turns out; this isn't always the case though. When an investor gets too involved in the details of a purchase, they fail to see the big picture. A savvy investor never gets invested in every minute detail about a property. While you are lengthening the whole buying process by doing this, the seller may just get another buyer who wastes no time in sealing the deal. Sellers are humans, meaning they are likely to get irritated of all the nitpicky questions you are asking about a property. Do not overanalyze a property by focusing on a small subset of issues that are of no major relevance to the deal in a bid to land the best deal possible.

2. Doing a Surface Due Diligence

This is basically the opposite of the first mistake and it refers to not getting all the important information you need before making a purchase. There are two ways of making this mistake: the first is not reviewing the previous operating statements and current rental income carefully. The operating statements usually contain a lot of important information. The second is performing a cursory inspection of the property. When buying a property, you need to bring an inspector over to check every unit, space, and area in the building, laundry areas and crawlspaces included.

3. Not knowing the market phase at a particular moment

There are four market phases which most new investors don't know: recovery, expansion, hyper-supply, and recession. During the recovery phase, the market usually experiences reduced vacancy and no new construction; this is the best phase for buying the 'right' properties. However, it is usually hard to get any loan during the market recovery phase. The expansion phase is one where there is a declining vacancy and new construction, with an expansion of rent and occupancy. Vacancy increases and there are new constructions in the hyper-supply market phase while in the recession phase, there is usually a quick decline of occupancy and rental rates. Most new investors think commercial real estate only appreciates and they could just buy property to hold on for a long time so it would appreciate. However, whether you buy and hold on to your property or not should depend on the current market cycle.

4. Insufficient knowledge of market and demographics

Whether you are a newbie to the industry or not, market and demographics are two things you should never make the mistake of being ignorant of. Always understand the market and demographics of any place where you are buying property because just having a property in the market doesn't guarantee success. Ensure you understand all key metrics which you can use to rank the market when there is a need. These include employment rate, job growth, population growth, unemployment, tenant rates, etc.

5. Not understanding rents and property values

Cap rate, debt coverage ratio, cash on cash return, etc. are all important terms you should get very familiar with because these are what you use to determine a building's rents and property values. Not knowing how to value a property or the market rate could result in overpaying for a property.

6. Being ignorant of the asset type

Many new investors in the commercial real estate market make the mistake of not research about the types of property in CRE because they assume it's the same as residential real estate. Even if you have had previous experiences in the residential market, commercial real estate is different and also has different property types. Ensure you get yourself familiar with the different property types ranging from office and retail to industrial.

7. Falling in love with a property

This is a very common mistake most new investors make, especially when trying to purchase their first commercial property. As an investor, you should never let your emotions get in the way of business. Many investors have made this mistake, which resulted in them buying a property with little market value. You should only fall in love with the numbers because that is what commercial real estate investment is all about. In the case where you fall in love with the looks, aesthetics, or details of a property, ensure you pinch yourself and snap back to reality as soon as possible.

8. Not knowing how to negotiate properly

Never make the mistake of being a bad negotiator; if you are one, endeavor to learn how to be a better negotiator because this factor may affect you negatively or positively. When negotiating a deal, price shouldn't be the only factor you consider. Also, consider other things such as the seller's motivation level. Do not make a seller think you are desperate to purchase a property; because you aren't and you shouldn't be.

9. Lack of cash reserve

Always have sufficient cash reserves in case you need to attend to certain unexpected expenses; not having enough cash reserve is a very big mistake investors, both experienced and new, make but you don't have to make this mistake too. A cash reserve is especially important when you are buying retail and office properties. Whenever there is a steady cash flow, ensure you put some away for future needs.

10. Being inexperienced with commercial leases

If you do not know how to negotiate a commercial lease or what should be contained in there, you need to learn as soon as possible. Even if you are new to commercial real estate, making the mistake of not understanding commercial leases isn't something you should do. Some investors even prefer to go online and download free commercial leases; this is something you should never do. Make sure you have your own attorney to draft a proper lease, tailored for each tenant and get familiar with the terms, language, negotiation tactics, and marketing skills for commercial renters.

These are the top mistakes every commercial real estate investor should avoid making. Of course, you will make some mistakes along the course of your investment career but the mistakes you make should be ones you can learn from so you never make the same mistake again. Since you are relatively new to the market, you will learn more and more about commercial properties the more you deal and have new experiences with properties and the market.

Chapter 5

Due Diligence:
Everything You Need to Know

Due diligence is a critical part of any commercial real estate negotiation and acquisition; it is comprehensive, complex, and absolutely important. As an investor, you should never leave any stone unturned while negotiating a commercial property deal because you may end up making a huge purchase mistake. Due diligence also takes a lot of your time because it involves you doing a critical assessment of all documents to detect any red flag with the property, tenant relationships, title, and many other things like the physical condition of the said property.

Basically, due diligence can be referred to as the process of doing your homework on a commercial property you are purchasing an investment so as to ensure you have a good deal. When doing due diligence, you check, recheck, and double check every important information that would help determine if the property is a good, average, or bad deal for you. There are three main classifications in due diligence; physical, financial, and legal.

Physical Due Diligence

In other words, this literally refers to a thorough inspection of a property to pick out the places that may need repair immediately or over time. This is usually not something you can effectively do alone; it is more advisable to hire a professional property inspection company to get the job done for you. Physical assessment of a property can be argued to be the most important part of due diligence since physical mistakes are usually the ones which cost the most to repair and the usually affect the long-term value of a property. Getting an inspection company is one of the easiest part of doing your due diligence; you can simply ask your broker because he or she is more likely to be familiar with companies like this. If not, you can use a referral or simply online to check. A physical assessment of the asses to be purchased should include a review of the building type, occupancy, fire rating, age and condition of current systems, drainage and grades, soils, etc. so as to make necessary changes if needed.

Financial Due Diligence

When it comes to the financial aspect of conducting due diligence, you've got to work with a professional accountant with commercial real estate investment experience to work out if the property is within or out of your investment budget. Note that not all accountants have real estate knowledge or experience so do not just get any accountant; get an accountant that is familiar with your industry. Again, make sure he or she actually has experience of the commercial real estate industry and not just the real estate industry generally. In a case where the investment is one of your largest ever, then it is absolutely important that the accountant you hire is someone who knows their onions. The best way to get an experienced accountant is through referral, not online or through a company or anything else. Ask within your network and find out if anybody knows an accountant that has experience with commercial property purchase and investment. One thing about this financial aspect of due diligence is that you should never just take a seller's word for it. It's not being distrustful, but being careful to avoid mistakes that could have been avoided. Check and double-check every information, document, records, and books presented to you by the seller. Make sure you verify every detail in the documents and each financial statement in the records and documents. Also, verify every penny of the rental income and any money spent on the property.

Legal Due Diligence

This is usually done by an attorney with the inclusion of a reputable escrow company. Ensure you hire an experienced attorney to help inspect thing such as: defects on the survey and title, possible environmental problems, proper or improper use of the property, encroachment, and other potential deal killers. Also, get your attorney to thoroughly review and audit the tenant leases. The trick is that you aren't buying a property in real estate a investment, instead, you are purchasing the property leases. Therefore, all possible imposed contracts on the property must be checked and double-checked. Naturally, you have to get an attorney familiar with the commercial real estate investment scene because lawyers usually specialize in different areas. There are real estate attorneys and you can easily get one through referral. Local or not, the attorney should be familiar and experienced with the laws of the state in which the property is located.

Checklist of everything needed for Due Diligence

To make your work easier on you, here is a list of the important documents, financial statements, and records you need for comprehensive due diligence on a commercial property. In your transaction, you should ask the seller to incorporate everything contained in this checklist into the sale contract and also require that the period specified for the due diligence doesn't commence until the date the seller provides every of the information we will be listed below. As a potential buyer of a commercial property, you retain the right to access all the documents you need to start the comprehensive due diligence process.

- The current title policy or commitment on the property, which is in the possession of the seller, with all other related documents.
- A topographic study of the property, the most current ALTA survey, and a copy of the engineering plans, construction blueprints, and as-built drawings respectively, all of which are also in the control of the seller.
- A legal document containing the description of the commercial property.

- Zoning compliance certificate for the commercial property and all other zoning approvals, variances and any pending applications.
- Declaration of property's conditions, restrictions, covenants, reservations, and also easements.
- A copy of third-party engineering, environmental reports in possession of the seller. Appraisals, boring reports, soil testing, foundation reports, radon studies, etc. should also be provided by the seller.
- An accurate copy of every written lease and guaranty, including amendments, and a verification of oral leases and understandings if any.
- A report of all rental and other income, security deposits, common area maintenance, and real estate tax contributions paid by tenants in the property. This should also include a rent roll showing the current rental rate, previous rental rates, lease commencement and termination dates.
- Every security deposits and other money which any tenant or third-party is entitled to.
- Three years real estate tax bills copy, including incentives and special assessment, every tax protest copies, correspondence and protest results, and previous property's utility bills' copies.
- Complete copy of each service contract (written), together with amendments if any. Complete and credible copy of every oral service contract with copies of all other contracts

and agreements concerning the property's operation, maintenance, and repair.

- A record of all income and expenses relating to the asset, including tax statements and collection reports for the past three years.
- A list of all personal property of the seller located at the property, in connection with the operation and maintenance of the property to be purchased, if any.
- A list of every permit, certificate of occupancy, government notices, warranties, code violations, special assessments, and valid guarantees and copies in seller's control
- Copies of existing insurance policies, certificates, and pending claims against the property.
- A pending litigation schedule, which may be affecting the seller's ability to release the property for purchase.
- Any other information, document, or record that you as the purchaser deem necessary for the process of due diligence and transaction, regarding the property and the status of its title.

Ensure to work together with your attorney, broker and accountant to verify that every part of the due diligence process was duly attended to. Remember that due diligence is a necessary and vital part of any commercial real estate property acquisition.

Chapter 6

How to Send Offers to Sellers and
Successfully Negotiate a Deal

An offer in commercial real estate investment is a written declaration of intent sent to a seller to make your interest as a serious buyer in the purchase of a property known. As a beginner, it can be pretty exciting and frightening when you want to send your first offer to purchase a commercial property. You want to make sure you get everything right; including the legal parts. So, we have of course prepared a breakdown of the steps you are meant to follow when making an offer for a commercial property.

Firstly, there are two ways to make your offer; through a letter of intent or a purchase contract. As a newbie, you probably won't know whether you should make your offer with a simple Letter of Intent or a fully detailed purchase contract. Usually, the letter of intent is used to notify the seller of your interest in the property as a serious buyer who is willing to close a deal fast with all the terms and price slated in the letter as long as both of you can work through all the details to fully complete the transaction. On the other hand, the purchase contract is the actual, final document which all the parties involved in a transaction sign to create a binding contract and agreement. It contains all of the legal clauses and addendums with a very detailed explanation of the transaction.

Many investors would rather present an offer with a basic letter of intent first since they don't want to put in time and effort to create a purchase contract for a property, which they don't have real feelings for or know the motivation level of the seller. So, a letter of intent is basically used to test the waters first i.e. ascertain whether the seller is motivated or not. The LOI shows the seller your interest in a property with the terms you are proposing and if the seller is interested I your terms, you can talk some more and see if you can both arrive at a deal. To make the seller understand that you may be really interested in purchasing the property, work with your attorney to draft a letter of intent that contains some clauses that creates a good faith expectation on both yours and the seller's sides.

A letter of intent is more advisable for presenting a first offer, especially because of the simple manner in which you are able to get the most important points across to the seller. In fact, the seller may find it quite convenient reading a simple one-page letter of interest than a 10-15 pages documents with all the legal clauses and terms that would make them bring in their attorney for a look together; the letter of intent is much easier to read and agree with immediately than a detailed purchase contract. However, the disadvantage of a letter of intent is that you don't have a legally binding contract and the seller may decide to cancel or go with another buyer at any point of the discussions. Therefore, you must make the effort to convert a letter of intent to an actual contract as soon as possible, especially of the property is one you are really interested in. When drafting up the letter of intent for sending your offer, it is imperative that you use a state-approved commercial contract for buying and selling real estate so the seller can see that you are in for serious business; most buyers feel more comfortable with the state-approved commercial contract.

Once you have sent an offer, the transaction comes to the negotiations part and this is where you need some pretty important tips to help you ensure you are on top of the game. Good negotiations skills are an integral part of commercial real estate transactions. When you have a motivated seller and some vital negotiation skills, you will always be able to make the seller agree to the terms and prices you are proposing. In fact, how good you are at negotiation could determine whether a buyer continues a transaction with your or simply moves on to another interested buyer.

Tips for negotiating a deal

Negotiations can be pretty intimidating when you are purchasing your first commercial property. Deal making and negotiations are more of art than science and you have to master this art. There are tenets of negotiations that you stand to benefit from as a commercial real estate investor. Here are 5 important tips for successfully negotiating a deal;

- **Do your homework**

Before you meet for a negotiation with a seller, ensure you already know everything there is to know about the property, the seller, and other related information that highlights what you have in front of you. Be familiar with all the important facts even more than the owner if needed.

- **Have a plan**

It is important to have a game plan before you start negotiating your first commercial property purchase. Know the key points you want to target during meetings with the seller and also the outcomes you want these meetings to have. You should already have the price, terms, and possible changes outlined before the negotiations start. Be straightforward and specific.

- **Stay in control**

Never let the seller dictate the tune of the negotiation; always be in control of the discussion because you are the one who really needs the deal. Brush up on your communication and persuasion skills and learn how to handle negotiations yourself. Also, never let anybody else do the negotiations for you; it should be your primary responsibility. If you are going to let someone else handle the negotiations for you, this should be your lawyer or broker and you must ensure their competence level is topnotch.

- **Find out the seller's motivation**

This doesn't mean asking them a direct question about why they are selling the property. Rather, it means listening and looking subtly for clues through the course of your discussions. Every investor wants the best possible deal they can get and a seller's motivation plays an important part in determining how great a deal is. Bridge the imaginary gap between the seller and yourself and don't be afraid to ask questions politely if you feel like they aren't really telling you anything.

- **Be empathetic and accommodating**

Usually, empathy isn't considered to be part of the skills required in succeeding in the commercial real estate industry. However, being empathetic about your counter-party's needs and goals can come in handy as your number one biggest deal making asset. Talk to your brokers. Also, be accommodating towards a seller, especially when you know the reason why they are selling the property. Make sure they are settled in before you begin the meeting; be encouraging, motivating, and easy to work with. Let them feel your empathy and sincerity. No matter how heated the discussion gets, maintain an air of pleasantry. Sellers prefer to work with people who make working with them as easy as possible.

After successfully negotiating and mutually agreeing to a deal, the next step is to close the deal and become the owner of your new property. So, let's take a look at how to successfully close a commercial property deal.

HOW TO PROPERLY CLOSE A DEAL

Once negotiations go well and your offer is accepted by a seller, the next stage is the closing of a deal that is usually a lengthy period; it takes between 30-90 days on average. Until the closing process is over though, it is not ideal to get overexcited about the deal. There are important actions to take to ensure that closing goes as smoothly as it can. Aside from signing the closing documents, it is also necessary for you to make sure the purchase is legal, final, and with a legal seal of approval. Before you can officially call the property yours, you will still need to pay a considerate amount of attention to the whole process.

ESCROW

Creating an escrow agreement between you and the seller is the first step to take after an offer is accepted. This is quite similar to a residential closing process where both parties have an escrow agreement to ensure seriousness and trustworthiness with the sale process. In escrow, a third party neutral to the whole transaction holds the closing fund in an account inaccessible to both you and the seller. Until all criteria in the deal agreement are met, the money will stay put in the escrow account. If one party decides to exit the deal through all the terms stated in the agreement, the funds can also be released. The criteria to be met are usually agreed on by both you, the buyer, and the seller. Compared to residential real estate deals, commercial property deals are even more closely monitored by the buyer, seller, and escrow agent during escrow. There are very little regulations to preventing one party from hurting the financial security or reputation of the other so both parties must work toward protecting their own investments. Title agents are usually the ones to act as the neutral third party to serve as an escrow agent between you and the seller.

TITLES AND CLOSING DOCUMENTS

Each of the parties participating in the deal must apply their best efforts in protecting themselves from being played. This process of doing their best is referred to as due diligence, which we have already covered above. As the buyer, you should ask the seller to present relevant documents to verify that the property is insured and in accordance with local laws and ordinances. Together with their attorneys, both buyer and seller should thoroughly review the contract of sale and ensure that every detail has been executed with no outstanding ownership or legal disputes regarding the property.

RENEGOTIATION

While inspecting the documents, property, and generally doing your due diligence, talk to the seller, ask questions, and start renegotiation if you find something that is out of place. Renegotiations are important for reviewing parts of the clauses that you are no longer comfortable with based on whatever you notice in the review of necessary documentation.

SIGNING OF DOCUMENTS

After thoroughly reviewing all of the documentation to make sure there are no stones left unturned, the documents become ready for signature and notarization. Apart from the title and insurance policy, you should also remember to take possession of all leasing documents; this is to allow you to benefit from while being held responsible for any breach of contract subsequently. An attorney and the title agent should also review all documentation to ensure nothing is missed in the whole process.

COORDINATE CLOSING REQUIREMENTS

Often, when closing nears, there may be new, unexpected issues which arise and needs attending to. The reason why issues often arise towards the end of closing is because of reliance on an independent third-party and the process of providing certifications and showings dated very closely to closing. As closing approaches, ensure that your broker, attorney, and other representatives remain available to respond to possible changes, demands, and arising circumstances.

CLOSING DAY

The closing day is when you officially become the owner of the new commercial real estate of the property. A part of the closing document on the closing day is a quitclaim or special warranty deed; this is the official document that transfers ownership of a property from a seller to the buyer. The deed usually accompanied by a title affidavit.

Commercial real estate investment has a more complicated, complex, and long closing process than residential real estate. Since there is very few regulations by the government regarding the process, both parties involved must do everything in their individual capacity to structure the deal, the closing documents and also ensure that the process goes as smoothly as possible by exerting good due diligence. Due to the large amount of capital usually involved and the varying sources of capital for investment, an independent third-party escrow account is used for the transaction process. While commercial real estate closing is typically longer than that of residential, there are more means of resolving disagreements in commercial real estate than residential.

Always consult with your attorney through the whole process of purchase i.e. from sending offers to closing the deal.

Chapter 7

Commercial Real Estate Financing

Commercial investment isn't a venture you can single-handedly finance unless you have a huge load of cash stacked away somewhere in your bank or safe. If you are one of those without cash stacked away, you need to understand how financing and loans work in commercial real estate investment. Commercial real estate loans differ from residential real estate's in many ways since it is a larger enterprise. To get financing for your investment, you must learn the different types of loans available for you; the loan requirements, how to find the best lender for you, and a comprehensive overview of what commercial real estate financing is all about which is what this chapter aims to explain to you in-depth, with the use of simplified and familiar commercial real estate terms.

Firstly, you may want to know the definition of property loan as relative to commercial real estate. Commercial property loans are simply mortgages delegated specifically to buyers of commercial properties. The kind of properties considered commercial are the ones that produce income and are used only for business activities, as you already know. This means before you can qualify for commercial real estate loans as an investor, you must be trying to purchase a commercial property only e.g. retails, office spaces, multi-family apartments, etc.

To purchase property, there are many real estate financing options that we will be examining to choose from. But, you must be prepared to guarantee the mortgage via collateral or in more technical terms, a lien. After getting the mortgage, the inability to meet all repayment conditions of the commercial property will result in the creditor or mortgage lender seizing the property. One important thing to also note is that commercial investment loans are only granted to businesses and not individuals. So, you must first register as a business entity in the form of a corporation or a limited liability company. This is one of the obvious differences between residential real estate and commercial real estate.

FINANCING OPTIONS FOR COMMERCIAL REAL ESTATE

To understand how financing works in commercial real estate, you require a basic knowledge of the property financial options in the commercial investment industry. You must also be able to tell which of these options the right one for your investment is. Apart from helping to finance the purchase of a property, commercial property loans could also help fund any construction projects, if there is the need. In addition, you as an investor can leverage your commercial property financing to keep your property fully maintained and operational so you can fully lease them out.

Below are different commercial real estate financing options offered by banks, insurance companies, private lenders, pension funds, and the U.S. Small Business Administration.

- **Conventional Bank Loan**

A large part of commercial real estate loans were developed by banks and these banks always prefer to lend money to people with strong credit histories. This is also referred to as the traditional commercial real estate financing option. If you are the type with a credit score of at least 660 and your plan is to work with mid-to-large-sized projects, a conventional bank loan is one of the viable options for financing your commercial property deal. A good thing about banks is that they do not require you to occupy the property and they always offer very competitive interest rates i.e. they borrow you the most money at the lowest cost. But, what they do require is a 20 percent down payment. In addition, they will likely charge a penalty if the loan gets paid off early. Conventional bank loans are, however, more suitable for the biggest credit borrowers and businesses with a healthy history of profit making over the course of a few years.

- **SBA Commercial Real Estate Loans**

There are two types of loan offered by the U.S. Small Business Administration and these are the SBA 7A Loan and SBA 504 Loan. These are some of the least expensive loans you will find anywhere for commercial real estate investment with a guaranty of repayment of a portion of the loan. SBA-backed loans are helpful in the sense that they increase a borrower's credibility and reduce risks for a lender.

The SBA 7a loan is the general purpose loan, which you can use for different business purposes, including the purchase and repair of commercial properties. It has a 25 year term for real estate with interest rate in a 7 to 9.5 percent range. This type of SBA loan is more useful for smaller projects and is the quickest to secure. Although it has a higher interest rate than the 504, it is the most popular loan option among the two.

On the other hand, you also have the SBA 504, which is more suitable for larger investment projects. With the SBA 504, the borrower is required to bring 10 percent of the loan amount as down payment while 40 percent of the loan is sourced from a certified development bank of the SBA. The rest of the loan is sourced from a lender; lenders usually favor loan requests which are backed by the Small Business Administration. SBA 504 loans work best for commercial investment projects valued at $1 million or more.

- **Hard Money Loan**

This is the kind of loan you get from private money lenders and investors and it is best reserved for when you are looking for a quick solution to some commercial real estate financing problem. Hard money lenders are known for offering short-term loans with a high interest rate and they do not evaluate a loan based on the borrower's credit history. Rather, the loan is evaluated based on the potential value of the property you are making an investment in. However, qualifying or accessing a loan with a hard money lender is usually easier than getting from the bank. In fact, as a beginner and a small business, it is best to start your first few commercial real estate investment projects with loans gotten from hard money lenders. Most investors only use hard money loans to quickly finance a short-term deals while negotiating a bigger loan with longer terms with a bank. Sometimes, hard money loans are referred to as bridge loans, but there is really another source of financing regarded as commercial bridge loans.

- **Commercial Bridge Loans**

Commercial bridge loans are short-term commercial property loans which you can hurriedly borrow to capitalize on an investment opportunity or purchase a property. Once it is time to repay the loan, you either pay off the whole loan in full or refinance it to a longer-term loan. Bridge loans "bridge the gap" between seeing a property you want to buy/renovate and getting an affordable, longer-term financing option. You can get commercial bridge loans either from the banks or hard money lenders. The interest rate will differ depending on whom you are borrowing from i.e. bank or private money lenders.

- **Commercial Real Estate Crowd-funding**

This is a somewhat recent entry to the list of financing options for commercial real estate investors. On crowd-funding platforms, many people lend small amounts of money toward your project and when you add all this money together, you will have a really huge commercial real estate loan ready for your investment. These crowd-funding platforms are, however, quite similar to hard money lenders due to the terms and cost.

- **Joint Venture Loan**

In the case where you are unable to secure commercial loans for your investment project or you simply don't want to bear the risk alone, you can opt for a joint venture loan. This is the type of financing where two or more properties apply for financing through a joint venture loan. With this type of loan, involved parties usually share the risks and returns in the commercial investment equally. A joint venture loan, however, ties the involved parties together based solely around one particular property; parties are not required to enter into a true commercial real estate partnership. Joint venture loans are best applied for with people you know and trust at least a little.

- **Online Marketplace Loans**

Also referred to as "soft money loans," these online marketplace loans have become one of the more popular financing options in commercial real estate investment. They typically involve getting matched with private investors who are ready to help finance commercial properties on an online marketplace. They are referred to as soft money loans because the interest rates are typically higher than that of the conventional banks but lower than that of hard money lenders or crowd-funding platforms. You can get shorter-term loans ranging from 6 months to a couple of years on online marketplaces. They are worth a shot when you have a quick short-term project to invest in.

These are some of the most popular and reliable means of securing financing for your commercial real estate investment projects. But, how does lending really work in commercial real estate? What are the requirements? Let's talk some more below.

How do Commercial Real Estate Loans work?

Residential real estate investors who are new to commercial real estate investment always assume that lending in residential and commercial real estates are the same but as we have ascertained, there are many differences that set them apart. It doesn't matter if you already have knowledge about how financing and loans work in residential, you must learn about how commercial real estate loans work if you want to be a successful commercial property investor.

The first difference between commercial real estate loans and that of residential is the individual/entity aspect of borrowing. While you can apply for loan as an individual in residential real estate industry, you can only borrow commercial loans a registered business entity which is created specifically for the purpose of purchasing and owning commercial real estate. You may register the entity as a corporation, developer, LLC, limited partnership, trust, and even funds. Now, as an entity, you may not necessarily have a financial track record or credit rating before you can apply for CRE loans. However, lenders will often require a guarantee in the form of a lien for the loan. A lien is the legal right to take over a property if an obligation isn't discharged, meaning the lender will take over your property if you are unable to meet the terms of the loan. This is usually referred to as a non-recourse debt. You can also provide the lender with an individual or group of individuals to serve as guarantor; he or she is liable to pay the loan in the eventuality of a default.

Loan repayment is another way in which commercial real estate differs from residential real estate. The repayment length for a commercial loan is typically between 5 to 20 years with a longer scheduled periodic payment period. For instance, if a lender makes a commercial loan term eight years, the scheduled periodic payment period may be between 20 to 30 years. In this case, the borrower makes payments of a certain amount for eight years based on the loan he or she is repaying over the 20 to 30 years period. After this, a final payment of the whole amount left on the loan balance is made. The length of the scheduled periodic payment will typically affect the amount of interest charged by a lender on a loan. If the borrower has a strong credit score, he or she may negotiate the terms of the loan with the lender. What this means is that the longer the repayment length is, the more the interest charged on a loan. On the other hand, residential loans are scheduled for loan repayment in periodic installments over an agreed period of time.

Commercial real estate is also different from residential real estate based on the loan-to-value ratio. Simply referred to as the LTV, this is a figure that represents the value of a loan against a property's potential value. The LTV is calculated by dividing the loan amount by the property's purchase price or the potential value, usually the lower of the two. Lenders often give investors with lower loan-to-value ratio more robust rates than they give investors with higher LTVs. This is because investors with lower LTVs mean lesser risks for the lender. The average acceptable LTV for commercial real estate is usually between 65 to 80 percent while residential loan lenders may accept LTV of up to 100 percent. The LTV accepted by commercial loan lenders is determined by the loan category.

The Debt Service Coverage Ratio is another thing commercial real estate lenders consider when determining the terms and rate of a loan. The DSCR determines a property's ability to pay its debts by comparing the NOI with the annual mortgage service. DSCR= NOI/annual mortgage service. A DSCR of below 1 percent portrays an unfavorable cash flow. Therefore, lenders will only give loans to investors with a DSCR of at least 1.25; this is to ensure favorable cash flow. However, they sometimes accept lower DSCR for loans with shorter periodic payment schedule and properties with reliable cash flow like retails and offices. Higher DSCR ratios are required for properties with unpredictable cash flow e.g. hotels and resorts since they usually have short-term leases unlike other commercial real estate properties.

Interest rates for commercial loans are generally higher than that of residential loans. Commercial real estate also often involve certain fees which add to the overall weight of the loan, including loan application, appraisal, legal, survey fees, and loan origination.

Before the loan is approved or worse, rejected, you will be required to pay some cost upfront while others simply apply naturally. Then, there is the prepayment aspect; commercial real estate loans usually have restrictions on prepayments, in a bid to preserve a lender's expected yield on a loan. If you repay a loan before the maturity date, you may have to pay prepayment penalties. The four types of exit penalties include; prepayment penalty, interest guarantee, lock out, and defeasance. The prepayment penalty is the basic type because lenders simply multiply your current outstanding balance by a specified payment penalty. With interest guarantee, the lender is entitled to an agreed amount of interest whether you pay off the loan early or not. Lockout makes it impossible for you to pay off a loan for a specified period of time, for instance, a 10-year lockout. Defeasance refers to a substitution of collateral. Rather than paying cash to the lender, you are required to exchange new collateral, which is usually the U.S. Treasury securities for the original collateral put in place for the loan. This may reduce fees, but it normally has a high very penalty attached for paying off a loan early. Lenders often specify the prepayment terms in the loan document and as with other loan terms in commercial real estate, you can negotiate with the lender. The amount of capital you receive for a commercial real estate loan is usually determined by the value of the property in question and the kind of lender you are working with.

How to Qualify for Commercial Real Estate Loans

To qualify for a commercial real estate loan, you must have some pretty important things in your credentials. Without these things, you may find qualifying for a loan almost impossible. Loan requirements for commercial real estate normally differ depending on the lender you are borrowing from. Here is a brief overview of three important requirements buyers will consider before they approve your loan application form and grant you access to a commercial real estate loan for your investment purpose;

- **Credit Score**

This is usually a basic requirement for any type of business loans and commercial real estate isn't excluded. The commercial loans you can qualify for usually rely heavily on your credit score. Naturally, lenders generally prefer to work with investors with a proven record of timely loan repayment and well-managed finances. To ascertain this, lenders consult your personal credit score and business credit score, respectively. There is no fixed credit score required to qualify for commercial real estate loans but lenders generally have a progressive range. Hard money lenders are the easiest loan lenders to access and they typically set their required credit score at around 550. If you have a credit score of 700 and above, you will have access to the best of loans like the SBA and conventional bank loans available to you.

- **Collateral Value**

Commercial real estate lenders, especially hard money lenders don't just look at your personal and business finances when considering you for a commercial real estate loan; they also consider the property you are purchasing or renovating.

Commercial real estate loans are asset-based loans, which means the property itself usually act as collateral for the loan. Therefore, lenders consider the collateral value when determining if you qualify for a loan or not. If you are unable to pay off the loan, the lien on the property gives the lender the legal rights to seize and sell off your property in order to satisfy the debt. This is something we have reiterated over a few times so you can know how crucial to commercial real estate financing it is. Since the property is central to the loan agreement and can affect lenders' loan security, lenders will want to make sure they have a full evaluation and appraisal of the property to see whether it can sufficiently cover the lender's assets. This is a basic requirement for borrowing in commercial real estate investment. If your plan is to do a complete renovation, lenders will also consider the after-repair value (ARV) of the property. Some lenders may base the loan amount you qualify for on the ARV of the property.

- **Length and Time of Business**

Commercial real estate lenders generally require you to know the length of your time in business before they approve a commercial property loan for you. This may be a simple thing, but it can have significant implications on the amount of loan you qualify for. The younger a business is, the riskier a lender considers it. Someone who has a business that has been around for some time has proven that they can manage a business to effectively withstand all the ups and downs that accompany managing a small business. This makes the lender certain that this person will be able to repay a loan. Your business must have been operating for at least two years to have the potentials of qualifying for a commercial real estate loan. Lenders sometimes consider management experience too before issuing investors commercial loans. Having a considerable amount of experience in running and developing a business brightens your application in the eye of the commercial real estate lender because it proves you are an ideal candidate for a loan.

Also, take a look at this list of required documents for loan application;

- Purchase contract
- Property address and description
- Property market analysis and business plan
- Budget for property
- Environmental reports
- Existing property's conditions
- Scope of work for renovation
- Last three years personal tax returns
- Personal credit report
- Records of personal sources of income
- Percentage of owner-occupancy
- Square footage of the property

Providing a complete application with all necessary documentation enables the lender the opportunity to quickly review your loan application and hopefully approve it. The more responsive you are to requests for information, the better your chances of getting the lender to approve your loan and charging you a lower loan rate.

STRATEGIES FOR GETTING THE BEST LOAN

Even when you understand all the methods of getting commercial real estate financing and the requirements, you still need additional knowledge of the best strategies to use in applying for a loan and getting a very good rate. Commercial real estate beginners often assume that the loan qualification process is an easy one because lenders are meant to lend money after all. This is true in part, but you also need strategies to not only ensure the whole loan application process goes smoothly, but to also make sure you get the best deal available i.e. friendly loan terms and rate. Apart from preparing all necessary documentation for loan application as we have already looked at, below are some strategic tips you can employ when applying for a loan.

- **Have a proper plan**

Lenders usually want to review and understand a borrower's business or property strategy: why does a borrower want the loan and how exactly would the loan improve the value of a property or increase the borrower's income? These are the questions you should explicitly answer in your property strategy. Always keep your strategy to mind when meeting with your loan officer. Be straightforward and direct; never waffle from the point of the meeting. This will increase your chances since your loan officer will recognize that you have a serious-minded strategy in place.

- **Develop a corporate structure diagram**

As a real estate investor, you will definitely have multiple corporate structures, which are often complex. These could range from family trusts, associated businesses, and special purpose property vehicles to self-managed superannuation funds. Creating a clear and accurate diagram of your corporate structures avails a lender the opportunity of understanding your business structure at a glance and this could save you weeks in reduced loan approval period since the lender can easily understand your business structure from the go.

- **Create a current rental schedule**

A detailed rental schedule with current information about tenants can also play a big part in improving the possibility of getting your loan approved. A rental schedule or tenancy schedule as it is also referred to normally details information about what tenants pay as rent so that an investor can properly determine a property's income value. A rental schedule should contain: tenant's form, part of property occupied, type of business, rental rate, commencement of the lease date, lease expiry date, terms of the lease, and rate of outgoings paid. Tenancy schedule varies by gross rents, turnover rents, and net rents depending on the commercial property type.

- **Study comparable sales**

Before you go on and apply for a loan, ensure you first study the comparable property assets in locations close to the property you are trying to purchase. Applying for a loan with comparable property asset information can increase your chances of getting very good loan deal because the lender would see you as someone with specialist knowledge of commercial property and its competitive analysis of its operation environment. This scores a level of respect with the lender and this could be greatly helpful to your loan approval process.

- **Apply with a property cash flow**

A property cash flow of two to three years can give a lender a lot of information about your property if you provide it. This could be really helpful in letting a lender or loan officer understand your future perspective of the property and your perspective on issues such as tenancy vacancies and capital expenditure.

- **Set your terms first**

Once you provide every requirement needed for the loan request and you know you have a good standing with the lender, never let him or her dictate the terms of the loan agreement first. Always set your terms first. When lenders set terms first, they usually set it so high that it becomes quite difficult to beat it down. Therefore, be the one to put the front foot first by telling the lender the interest rate you expect right from the start of the discussions; make sure you tell the lender what establishment fee you will pay too. Then, the lender would be the one to try to push the terms up. One surprising thing about this is that many lenders don't usually try to push the terms up when the borrowers set the loan terms first.

If you carefully read and assimilate all of the information presented in this chapter and you consistently put every tip into practice, you will in no time become a master of securing the best financing for your commercial real estate investment projects. Financing is a critical and integral part of investment that you should strive to understand as much as possible.

Chapter 8

Other Means of Financing Commercial Real Estate Investments

Apart from the more common financing options we discussed in the previous chapter, there are other multiple ways of getting financing for a commercial real estate investment project, but these options are not known to many investors. If you are looking to stray from the more conventional means of financing commercial real estate projects, below are some other interesting, non-traditional and viable lending and financing options you can explore.

- **Private Lenders**

This doesn't refer to the hard money lenders; rather, it refers to individuals with access to substantial capital and a willingness to invest the capital in a profitable business. This could be a close friend or even someone you meet at a networking event or group. From the name "private lender," these people aren't licensed or institutionalized to lend money but they do so with the intent of making their investment capital back, with interest. It is way easier to meet a private lender and get them to accept your loan application. However, the loan duration is usually very short and the cost of interest rate is typically around 12 to 15 percent, which is a whole lot of interest rate.

- **Venture Capitalists**

Another set of people whom you can seek a commercial investment loan from are the venture capitalists. These are individuals with very high net-worth and corporations with interest in investing in start-ups that show huge potentials. Like private lenders, venture capitalists also have no official authorization for lending money but they are always willing to lend out more than you would get from a traditional small-business loan. However, they are usually very selective in nature, making it harder to get loan approval. To get a commercial investment loan from a venture capitalist, you are going to have to ensure that your investment really does have potentials.

- **Angel Investors**

Another source of commercial real estate financing, angel investors are well-to-do individuals who typically provide funding for new business ventures with potentials, usually in exchange for ownership equity or convertible debt. In clearer terms, they partly acquire a part of the business. These types of lenders are always willing to take more risks in a business if they feel it has very huge potentials. However, you cannot technically refer to money gotten from an angel investor as a loan since they just acquire part of the business. Before you apply for financing from an angel investor, make sure it is really what you need for your venture.

- **Micro Loans**

Micro loans are a source of small loans usually around $50,000 even though people rarely take as much as that when they apply for a micro loan. These kinds of loans are good for when you need to attend to something urgently in a property or if you have a really quick and small deal to close. Although micro loans are more accessible than traditional loans, there is the possibility that it would not cover all of your needs, as a loan should.

- **Money Partners**

Like the name portray, these are people you partner with because of their access to funding. This type of financing option is more feasible for you if you have little to zero capital because the money partner is always ready to cover the financial aspect of the commercial investment deals.

To find out about other possible sources of financing for your commercial real estate investment deal, consult with your experienced accountant and trusted broker. Before you choose a particular financing source, do your research and make sure that this particular lending source is suitable for your business.

SECONDARY FINANCING: WHAT IS IT?

Secondary financing is used to describe a situation where a property owner gets a second-mortgage on a property that already has one mortgage. With secondary financing, the first mortgage is given priority in settlement of claims. Usually, commercial real estate investors apply for a second mortgage in order to reduce the loan to value (LTV) ratio of the initial loan. However, most lenders generally forbid second mortgage on commercial properties because they fear that if cash gets tight, the property owner would rather use repair money to make payments on the second loan rather than maintaining the property like they should.

Chapter 9

How to Get Tenants
for Your Commercial Property

Acquiring commercial property is one thing; getting tenants to fill up the property is another thing. A commercial real estate investment would turn out unsuccessful if the owner is unable to fill up the space with tenants who are meant to pay the rent and generate good income for you. Tenants are the lifeblood of any commercial property investment and when you have the right tenants, you are stabilizing your property for long-term and also boosting the investment potential of the property.

Good tenants do the most for your investment over time, therefore, you must know how to get the best of tenants for your commercial property. To get the best tenants possible, you can create a database that focuses on connecting all of the local businesses i.e. potential tenants in your area or city. To do this, you need to apply logical leasing strategies; a process that requires logicality, systematization, and constant activity. From a leasing perspective, these strategies have plenty benefits to a commercial property owner. Understanding the activities and needs of local businesses around you from a property perspective helps you recognize the many leasing opportunities available in the local markets. Here are some of the ways through which you can find the best tenants for your new commercial property;

Business types should naturally be your main concern when filling up your space with tenants. Certain business types are more active than the others. Based on this, determine the businesses that are most important in order of the local market. Considering this, choose the businesses you are willing to lease to in an ongoing way. Understand the type of properties these businesses require and the improvements they may need. Using this, you can market your commercial leasing services specifically based on this. This means you create a target audience rather than the normal, general audience.

Reviewing other properties is another step to take when looking for renters for your property. Do a research of all commercial buildings in your precinct, specifically the better buildings with equally fitting quality tenants. Some of these tenants may be looking to relocate or move due to pressures of contraction or expansion. Over time, you may come to be recognized as a trusted property owner and the right choice when it comes to commercial property leasing around the local area. By doing this, you will be establishing correct business relationships which would help you greatly in the long term.

Reviewing other tenants is still another thing to do aside from the properties review step. Go through the streets in your location so as to discover exactly where tenants are and what comes to their mind when they think about property occupancy. Some tenants may have issues with their landlord or the property occupancy cost. Based on this, there would be plenty of reasons for them to want to relocate if they find a good property at the right time. For this very reason, ensure you stay in touch with them for whenever they are ready.

Seeking out expanding tenants is something you should make a priority if you really want to find tenants for your new property. There are buildings with certain limitations when it comes to future occupancy. The floor plates may be too small or the improvements made may be substandard. There are other reasons why tenants may want to move, apart from expansion. Do your research, tailor your property to accommodate these reasons, and leverage on them before other property owners can; use these to market your commercial leasing service.

Advertising is also one of the ways for you to get new tenants but it usually comes with certain costs. There are ways you can advertise your commercial leasing services into a location or a group of targeted tenants but the main thing is to choose the right media for the advert. Then, ensure you follow the results of your advertising so you can decide whether it is necessary and efficient or not.

Send Direct mails and brochures to market your leasing services using the postal service. These mails and brochures can be sent to businesses and multi-family tenants around your local area. Through this process, you can also quote nearby properties and current vacancies. Tell the potential renters about the vacancies available for negotiation in your property.

Creating a link between suppliers, manufacturers, and wholesalers is a leasing opportunity that can get you the best tenants immediately and over time. If you carefully, you will notice a pattern and relationship among manufacturers, suppliers, and wholesalers depending on the business types you are targeting. Most times, many of these businesses need to be conveniently located near one another.

Cold calling is an old but golden method you can use to attract new tenants to your commercial property. Using the business telephone book, call all local businesses regularly with the record of everything being constantly updated in your database; track your progress with the records kept. Through regular calls and conversations, you will definitely discover local businesses looking to mover for whatever reasons.

Send email dispatches as you continue to build your database. Classify contacts in your database into different segments according to groups and locations. This is a specific process that produces awesome results when regularly engaged in. Ensure the dispatch emails detail spaces available for leasing.

By using any of the strategies we have discussed, you can easily get new tenants to fill up your new property and start enjoying the fruit of your commercial real estate investment labor. Do not be discouraged if it seems like you aren't getting tenants despite putting in all of the efforts you can. Vacancy is sometimes low based on some intangible market factors. With consistency and diligence however, you will in no time start having an influx of good tenants to fill up every space in your commercial real estate building.

Chapter 10

Selling Commercial Real Estate

O ver time, as you become more experienced and financially successful in commercial real estate investment, you may want to start buying and selling commercial properties rather than just leasing them out. As an investor, selling properties should be easy for you since you are already acquainted with the whole process. Yet, it is necessary for you to get some things in order of you are going to be selling commercial properties. If you have never been a seller, it will probably be hard to know what to do even as an experienced property investor. For the purpose of this chapter, we will assume you are a commercial real estate investor looking to sell off a certain property. Now, as a commercial property seller, what do you need to know and do? Below, we take a look at some of the best tips to help you sell your property quicker and at the right price.

The first thing is to understand the irresistible power of **curb appeal**. Take a really good look at the exterior of the property. Would you say it is in very good condition? Are there things you can do to spruce up the whole look and feel of it? Perhaps you need to add a new layer of paint to refresh the whole appeal of the property? Curb appeal is super important in both commercial and residential real estate investment because it gives potential buyers or investors a first impression of the property, which you may not be able to subsequently change or influence. A property with an air of neglect will turn potential buyers away and affect the sale price. Just like residential real estate, ensure the property is in very desirable condition. Although looks aren't as major of a factor in commercial investment as it is in residential, it will still factor in, whether the buyer proceeds to inspect the property or not.

You should also develop a selling strategy just like you would have a strategy for purchasing a property. The easiest way to come up with an effective strategy is to use comp sales. This means looking for comparable properties close to your property and analyzing them. Your comparable properties analysis should include the location of the properties, how far they are from yours, the price the properties sold for, and the dates they were sold respectively. You may find this challenging since most of the commercial properties databases are not made available to the public. Nevertheless, try your best to get the information and use it to check out your competition. If you are able to find any properties for sale close to you, check them out and see what price they are selling for. Be especially attentive to the lease rates, location, and amenities. This will give you valuable insights into how you can step up to the competition. Comparable sales are great but nevertheless, investors/buyers will be interested more in the building's income rates, as you should already know.

As a buyer yourself, you should naturally understand the perspective with which a buyer purchases commercial property. Know the preferences of potential investors and tailor your terms around it. For instance, what could be the major feature an investor is looking for in a property? Are they looking for a turnkey property with 100% leases or are they looking to make improvements to the property and the leasing mix. Analyze your current tenant mix to figure out where you stand before fixing meetings and discussions with the investors. Let investors know the most important details; highlight the property and location's attributes. Include every notable cross streets located nearby your property. Also highlight the public transformation, highway proximity, and traffic generation numbers. Try to make information about demographics available to the investor because this type of information is typically helpful. Age, household income, and population are important demographics, which investors are always looking for.

Enlist the help of a professional broker. Of course, you can use the same broker you use for your purchase of commercial real estate since it's pretty much the same thing. The whole selling process can be as overwhelming as the buying process so it is okay to partner with a trusted broker to work with on the sale so as to alleviate the stress. The relationship you have with your broker is a critical one. The whole process of selling CRE is complicated and only a trusted broker can help you navigate through the process quite easily. Make sure your broker is an expert about the local market, employs the use of relevant CRE technologies, has a widely acknowledged reputation for always attracting qualified buyer, has a strong presence in the local market, possesses topnotch contract negotiation skills, and knows the best practices for market research.

Make conscious efforts to increase the value of your property by engaging in some activities that are geared towards increasing property value.

INCREASING YOUR PROPERTY'S VALUE

When you purchase a commercial real estate property, you should keep it in mind that there are ways you can go to enhance the looks of your property and increase the market rental value. Thus, when purchasing a property, the property's potential and important historical data should be two of the things you consider. The value of commercial real estate property is primarily influenced by the cash flow generated by the property. So, no matter the strategy you employ, you have the chance of increasing your cash flow, decreasing your expenses, and overall improving the equity and value of the property. Here are five strategic ways to increase a property's value so as to make the most out of commercial real estate investment.

1. Improve the Property

Improvements to commercial properties usually take the form of substantial rehabilitation and cosmetic improvements to enhance the aesthetic look of the building. Cosmetic improvements usually of the commercial property's involve the changes and used of strong cosmetics, new paint, new decors, and many more while a substantial rehabilitation is one that involves making some structural improvements or changes to a property. For instance, this may be something like changing the possible structural outlook of a shopping mall. Improving a property increases the value of the property for not just your tenants, but also for your private portfolio as an investor too. Making improvements make it possible for you to increase your current rental rates.

2. Increase Rent

Another way to improve the value of a commercial property is by increasing the rents. When looking at historical data provided on a property, find out of tenants are paying market rent or if there is a potential for a reasonable increment in rents. Find out how the improvements and changes you make can be used to back up your rent increase. Be attentive towards both the lower and upper levels of rents that are being charged for properties that have similar market characteristics so as to avoid pricing yourself out of the commercial real estate market.

3. Reduce Expenses

Review the historical operating statements of the property to seek out areas where you can s decrease the expenses. For instance, improving the property by changing to more energy efficient light bulbs in the common areas of a property can have a major impact on the monthly electrical bills which is which will surely enjoy a decline or decrease. Another example is to ask the gas company to individually meter the units in a property so that instead of paying for gas, you can simply pass on the responsibilities/expense onto the tenants. A commercial property owner can easily cut and decrease expenses without having any significant impact on the operations of the commercial property.

4. Change a property's intended use

Most times, the value of commercial real estate property can usually be drastically impacted by changing the intended usage of the property. For instance, if you purchase an old industrial warehouse in the center of a bustling areas, you can convert it to a hotel, office building, condo or any other commercial real estate property with potentials by seeking out the necessary zoning variance rather than just keeping it as the same old industrial warehouse which doesn't actually make sense for the location.

5. Add Amenities to boost return on investments

Apart from a general improvement to the outlook of the property, you can also add up amenities that would be of immense benefits to your tenants. These could include a fitness center, an automated coffee bar, bigger trade halls, and high-end conference rooms. These amenities can also be complemented with the addition of income producing roof space for large meetings, convention halls, and automated laundry machines.

These are techniques you can employ to facilitate changes that result in the increase of a commercial real estate investment property's value.

Chapter 11

Buying Commercial Properties through Bank Repossessions and Auctions

Buying commercial properties through bank repossessions means buying properties that were once being financed by banks but were defaulted on by the owners. Because of this, the bank takes back the property into its possession and then sells it off to someone else in order to make up for the amount of debt owed by the defaulter to the bank. Although bank repossession isn't something you wish for as a commercial real estate investor, it sure is something you can take advantage of to get some really good commercial investment deals. Most bank-owned commercial properties are for sale, however, it is still very important that you get some professionals to help you look into the property with thorough investigation so you can submit a competitive bid for the property.

Before you start your search for bank commercial properties, you must first recognize the type of property you are looking to purchase; this will help tailor your search and make it more specific. Are you looking for a retail building, office building, apartment building or any other type o commercial property? Once you know the type of commercial property you are looking for, get a list of banks' websites so you can check them up. Banks typically list the properties they have for sale on their websites. You can do this with the use of a search engine; simply go to your favorite search engine, such as Bing or Google. Then, type the name of the bank and "REO" into the search engine; immediately, you will see the results of some bank websites where their REOs are listed. For example, if you are looking for REO properties owned by Wells Fargo, you go to Google and type "Wells Fargo REO" and this brings up a result of the list of commercial properties Wells Fargo has up for sale. US Bank, Wells Fargo, and BMO Harris are some of the banks with REO properties in the United States. You may do a local search according to banks in your local area.

Another place where you can find bank commercial properties on for sale is Loopnet. This is a very valuable website that contains information about listings for bank owned commercial properties within the United States. To access the listings, you would have to sign up to be a member after which you get access to the site's premium bank-owned commercial property listing. The listings will typically contain the size, price, and type of commercial property which could be office, retail, residential, or more. Banks normally try to auction REO properties before listing them for sale so you should also check out local auctions around you. Monitor upcoming auction events in the newspaper so as to stay updated on the auctions holding around your local area or in an area within proximity to you. According to statistics though, most properties displayed at auctions are usually never bid on so, going to auctions is just a way of looking out for good commercial properties that will be on the market sooner or later. To make your chances of getting REO properties for sale, you should also work together with a trained commercial real estate broker. An experienced broker is more liable to have listing information that may otherwise be hidden to you. If you already have a broker, make sure he or she is competent but if you don't, ask around your networks for referrals on an experienced broker with extensive knowledge of commercial real estate or get one by using the phonebook to track brokers down.

Even when you are buying a commercial property from the bank, you must ensure you do your due diligence on the property. As is standard, the location of the property should be first and foremost in your check. Why was the initial owner unable to complete the loan repayment? Was the property located in an area with little or no potential and tenant appeal? The most appealing properties to tenants are those in a location with access to public transportation, visibility from the road, sufficient foot traffic, and nearby businesses. Consider if the businesses close to the building are compatible with your target clientele's businesses or do they pull in different clients? If the REO building is an apartment or multi-family, ensure you find out things like the condition of neighboring properties, and location of schools, hospitals, grocery stores, etc. After this, make sure you do a standard physical assessment of the property. Do not assume that this is unnecessary because it is a bank-owned property. Go with an inspector and contractor to determine the level of repairs needed and just how much these repairs would cost. Again, you can use your phonebook to look up building contractors. Since these buildings are usually occupied with tenants or abandoned, there is always some repair issue to take care of so ensure you are thorough in your inspection of the property.

Talk to the bank about the current tenants. Ask about the number of units in the building, the number of rented ones, and how long they have been occupied by each tenant. Also ask for the rent-rolls, which contain information about the complete number of tenants, names, and the terms of lease. If the bank isn't willing to provide this information, you could take it up a notch and try to contact the former owner; ask them nicely for the information you need. Before you pay for the purchase, analyze your rental income potential. What can you charge for rent? The bank i.e. the current landlord may not be charging a market rent, so do some research on what landlords in that particular area are charging. You can either collaborate with property management companies or go online to get this information. There are several sites that offer information. For example, padmapper.com. Also, ensure you do a comparable study of nearby buildings. Properties that are in a much better location will probably charge higher than the other properties. Importantly, ensure you ask the bank for available financial records. Since the property is a foreclosed one, there is every chance that the complete financial record won't be available. But, work with your broker using the available records to help calculate the right bid amount for the commercial property.

Now, it's time to make an offer for the REO property. You will need to work with your team of lawyer, accountant, and mortgage broker. If you can't single-handedly finance the transaction, you will need to apply for a loan using any of the financing options we have already discussed in chapter 8. You can opt to apply for a loan from the bank, which you are buying the property from; they may oblige or they may not. In fact, they may be the one to offer to finance the purchase, but if they don't, check any of the means of financing we looked at and choose a suitable one for the transaction. Get all the necessary documents and apply for a loan before you work on calculating the bid.

Together with your broker, sit and assess the bank's sale price for the property. Is it too high? Or is it too low? If it seems to be too low, then it probably means there is something wrong with the property and the bank is looking to have it offloaded. Ask your broker to study the real estate market in proximity and find out what a fair sale price would be. As a savvy investor, you may want to begin the offer with a low bid amount in a move to get the bank to negotiate. But, you should know every bank is different; most banks are not interested in getting anything below top dollars even if the property was foreclosed. Therefore, ensure you begin bidding with your best price. Ask your lawyer to help draft a purchase and sale agreement, which will be submitted to the bank. Since the agreement will become a legally binding contract if accepted, you should definitely use a lawyer. Send it in to the bank as soon as it is drafted. Make sure you include a feasibility contingency to review expenses, leases, income, market potential and other relevant issues before purchasing the property. Include an expiration date in your offers so as to figure out how long you will have to wait for an acceptance offer or a counteroffer from the bank. Put it in mind that banks rarely respond to offers quickly. If the bank responds with a counteroffer rather than an acceptance offer, you will proceed to the negotiations. Normally, they will send their own purchase and sale agreement, which might not completely be of benefit to you. Review the purchase and sale agreement with your broker and lawyer but know that banks are normally hard negotiations even when there is a motivation to sell; bring in your best negotiation skills.

Once you and the bank arrive at an agreement, do other important things such as a title search and then proceed to close the deal. Like that, you have been able to successfully purchase a bank foreclosed commercial property.

Advantage of Bank Repossessed Properties

There are many pros and cons of purchasing a foreclosed property; these benefits make purchasing REO commercial properties give you the possibility of getting very good deals, especially when the amount owed to the bank is less than the property's market value.

- Banks that have foreclosed properties on listings are usually not looking to make a profit on the sale; they just want to recoup the debt and their losses. So, you could find yourself a good bargain if you purchase a property listed as REO.
- The bank is a VAT vendor so there is no need for transfer duty payable on a foreclosed property.

119

- Banks always require the municipal accounts are up to date, so you don't have to worry about taking on somebody else's municipal debt.

Disadvantage of Bank Repossessed Properties

- Like we already said, most repossessed commercial properties are usually in very poor condition and they always require some level of renovation. As the buyer, you will need to consider the cost of renovation on top of the purchase price to ensure that the deal is really a good bargain or a potential money trap. Location is primary to any commercial real estate deal so never compromise on location just to get a seemingly good deal.

- If the property has tenants occupying the space, you as the new owner will be responsible for vacating the tenants from the property. Sometimes, this may be as simple as giving the occupants a quit notice or worse, it would be a long process of legal eviction which spells more stress for you.

- When purchasing a foreclosed property, there will probably be a lot of hassles and you should know if the whole stress is worth your while.

How does Bank Repossessions actually work?

When a commercial property owner can no longer meet their loan terms and they are in substantial arrears, the bank takes a legal action by serving the owner with a court summons, taking judgment, and attaching the property eventually. If the homeowner is still in arrears by the time of attaching the property, the bank will request the court sheriff to provide selling the property at a public auction event. At the auction, a bank representative is entitled to purchasing the home if the bids aren't enough to cover the outstanding fees owed to the bank. Thus, the home becomes a repossessed property or property in possession once it is 'bought back' by the bank at the auction. Immediately the bank purchases the property at the auction, it becomes the legal registered owner of the property. In this case, the bank either puts the property on sale so as to recoup their losses or rents it back to the former owner on a month to month basis lease agreement.

Tips for Purchasing Commercial Real Estate at Auctions

Buying properties at auctions is a great way of getting huge returns on your investment so use some of these tips to help you through the process of purchasing properties at auction events.

- Prepare the cash. Most action events require you to close the deal within a very short time after auction closing; this is usually around within 30 days. This makes it impossible for you to get traditional financing for the purchase of an auctioned property. So, ensure you have a credit line available or a lender willing to loan you on credit once the auction closes. Generally, the purchase agreements in auctions are not open to financing contingencies so if you can't prepare the cash for closing, you are at risk of losing your earnest money and there is also the liability of damages.

- Join the property tours. When it comes to auctions, this is usually the only time a potential buyer gets to see or inspect a property so you should never miss the property tours. Most auctions have specified dates available for the property tour; find out the dates and make it a date. When you do go on the tour, check out if the property has tenants you can ask about the units and issues they are facing. Look out for potential improvements and repairs to be made, if any.

- Request for the format of the auction. Auctions come in different formats and it is only right you know the format of the ones you attend. Get yourself familiar with auction types and their definitions; Online vs. Sealed Bid, Reserve vs. Absolute Auction, etc. There are various types depending on the company holding the auction.

- Be aware of insider bidding. Many times, auction companies get insiders to bid up a property on the auction being held. This is done to artificially inflate the bidding price of the property. Do not be pressurized into bidding a higher price than you can afford.

- Get experts to represent you at auctions. With most auctions, you are expected to do due diligence before the main event. Therefore, you need to have your team of broker, attorney, accountant, inspector, contractor, etc.

122

ready to go over all the materials presented and become comfortable with every part of it before purchasing. Make sure everyone on your team is good at what they do.

- Never infuse emotions into a purchase. It doesn't matter whether you like a property or not; if the deal isn't right, it isn't right. Know when you reach your limit; if you have a limit set, don't get too competitive and overexcited by trying to win the auction just to win. Auctions are usually very exciting and coupled with the possibility of a strong return on investment, they may get you overwhelmed. However, ensure you recognize and stick to your limits because there are always better deals waiting in the market.

These are the tips you can follow in getting bank repossessed and auctioned properties at a great price with a huge potential return on income. Auctions and repossession may be good sources of good commercial real estate deals. However, it is pertinent for you to know when to avoid making these type of deals. Before you make an offer for auctioned and repossessed bank properties, make sure you have adequately done all form of research and appraisal to verify that this deal is a good one for you. If it doesn't seem like a good enough deal, do not hesitate to move on to the next deal.

STAYING UP TO DATE WITH TRENDS IN THE MARKET

Keeping up with news and trends in the real estate market is a way of gaining insights into the state of the economy in a country. When you follow trends in the commercial real estate market, it opens up windows to other aspects of the nation's economy and social progression. Therefore, to be a savvy real estate investor, you must ensure you follow and stay up to date with trends in the commercial industry and the general market. Here are the best websites and online news outlets to help you on top of the news and trends in the commercial real estate industry. These include;

- Forbes: An established site about wealth and finance with sections dedicated to real estate and commercial real estate specifically.

- Realty Times: Here, you will find tips for improving your property and how to make the best financial decisions when buying and selling.

- RIS Media: Offers insightful information on government acts relevant to the real estate industry and social acts.

- Realtor.com: This is a source of social Internet information with helpful posts centered on current trends and events.

- Entrepreneur: Everything business, ranging from making money and doing smart business. They especially concentrate on real estate investment facts, news, and trends.

Conclusion

Congratulations, you have made it to the end of "Commercial real estate: the ultimate beginners guide for learning the effective ways in commercial real estate." We hope it was an interesting read and you have been able to absorb the wealth of knowledge on how you can build a successful commercial real estate investment career even as a newbie in the industry. This book has made efforts to intimate you with the most basic and technical knowledge you need to start investing in commercial properties, using simple language and relevant examples.

We looked at what commercial real estate is and the investment opportunities present for beginners in commercial real estate. We also discussed a range of commercial real estate topics to beef up your knowledge about commercial real estate substantially. Investment opportunities, property evaluation and appraisal, financing opportunities, and the best tips for landing great commercial property deals are just some of the new knowledge you now have from reading this book. In addition, we have been able to effectively educate you on important things such as offers, due diligence, negotiations, renegotiations, and closing of commercial real estate deals. More importantly, you have been taught the best strategies for effectively finding the right tenants for your new commercial property. This book has delivered on the promises made in the introduction by providing you with practical tips, examples, and scenarios to help you fully understand how commercial real estate investment really works. Remember that we said networking is an integral part of commercial real estate investment projects and also provide you with comprehensive guidelines on how to effectively create a vast and valuable network in the commercial real estate industry. Once you master everything you have been able to learn from this book and start putting them into practice, you will in no time become a top expert in matters relating to commercial real estate investment.

Commercial real estate may be complex and complicated as many people like to think. Yet, beyond that web of complexity is the opportunity to build a consistent source of income and start living the life you deserve. If you have been stalling kick-starting your commercial property investment career, now is the best time to make a bold move and charge for the top of the food chain. Take that bold step and get started on your wealth-making journey!

References

https://investinganswers.com/dictionary/c/commercial-real-estate

https://m.huffpost.com/us/entry/us_13310450

https://www.bdc.ca/en/articles-tools/money-finance/buy-lease-commercial-real-estate/pages/how-negotiate-effectively-when-buying-commercial-real-estate.aspx

https://www.linkedin.com/pulse/10-tips-getting-best-commercial-property-loan-michael-holm

https://www2.deloitte.com/us/en/pages/real-estate/articles/commercial-real-estate-industry-outlook.html

Made in United States
Orlando, FL
14 May 2022

17862932R00072